THE EARRING STYLE BOOK

making designer earrings,
capturing celebrity style,
and getting the look for less

STEPHANIE A. WELLS

POTTER
CRAFT

NEW YORK

Published in the United States by Potter Craft, an imprint of the Crown Publishing Group, a division of Random House, Inc., New York.
www.crownpublishing.com
www.pottercraft.com

POTTER CRAFT and colophon is a registered trademark of Random House, Inc.

Library of Congress Cataloging-in-Publication Data

Wells, Stephanie A.
  The earring style book : making designer earrings, capturing celebrity style, and getting the look for less / Stephanie A. Wells.
      p. cm.
  Includes index.
  ISBN 978-0-307-46393-7
  1. Jewelry making. 2. Earrings. I. Title.

TT212.W42 2010
745.594'2--dc22

2009051998

Printed in China

Design by La Tricia Watford
Photography by Marcus Tullis

Page 6: Frank Micelotta/Getty Images. Page 8: Asadorian/Splash News. Page 9: Nigel Parry/CPi Syndication. Page 141: clockwise from top, Stephen Lovekin/Getty Images; John Sciulli/WireImage; Armando Gallo/Retna Ltd./Corbis.

10 9 8 7 6 5 4 3 2 1

First Edition

ACKNOWLEDGMENTS

I would like to acknowledge and extend my heartfelt gratitude to the following persons,
who have made the creation of this book possible.

My amazing husband, Jared, whose love, support, friendship, humor, and
intelligence keep me happy and sane.

My fabulous parents, Harlene and David, who taught me to never be afraid,
who continue to be wonderful role models,
and whose tireless babysitting efforts gave me time to write.

My sister and best friend, Alisa, who was the first to believe I could design,
and who walked the streets of New York City to sell my first collection,
pounding the pavement just to get the pieces seen.
Thanks to her amazing publicity talents, Double Happiness Jewelry is now known all around the world.

To my sweet little love, Geffen, whose every waking moment is of happiness and exploration,
and whose zest for life and quest to understand the world inspire me.

To the ladies of Double Happiness Jewelry, Portia, Ann, Jessica, and Lindsay,
who are all amazing, strong, and smart women. Their ability to run brilliantly with any task
I throw at them continues to amaze and humble me. It is a true honor to work with these women.

To my two grandmothers, Anna and Sally,
whose friendship and life experiences continue to motivate me.

And, finally, I want to thank Random House and Potter Craft
for helping to spread the joy of creativity through this book.
I am very thankful and grateful to work with my amazing editor, Rebecca Behan,
whose meticulous attention to detail, ability to truly absorb, comprehend,
and help clearly explain brand-new concepts is astounding.
Grateful acknowledgment is given to Betty Wong, Chi Ling Moy, La Tricia Watford,
and all those at Potter Craft who believed in and worked on this book.

CONTENTS

INTRODUCTION

Singer Alicia Keys wears the Laurel earrings (page 68).

I love to wear earrings. They are usually the first thing I think about while getting dressed, even though they are the last thing I put on. Earrings are my personal billboard: They project to the world a message about who I am and what I'm feeling. If I wear my big, funky, curvy Osiris earrings, I am saying, "I am feeling fun, edgy, and confident—so watch out!" If I have to attend a business meeting—and am feeling classic—I might wear my smaller, more conservative Judy earrings. Translation: "I am taking this meeting seriously." Maybe I want some attention from my husband, or I am just feeling pretty—I will put on my dangly, boho-chic Gisele earrings and strut through my day.

I wear my earrings everywhere—to work, to yoga class, on shopping trips, and during nights out on the town. All by themselves, earrings can create a look that speaks volumes. Jeans and a simple white tank become a fabulous outfit when they are topped off with a standout pair of earrings. A simple black dress and classy chignon ooze excitement and sex appeal when worn with dramatic, sparkly earrings. Why? Earrings make statements. They are worn close to your eyes, and they get noticed. They usually have sparkle and move or swing when you walk. For all these reasons (and many more), they call attention to themselves—and to you.

With clothing and accessories, society dictates certain norms: A business meeting means studs, while a night out means hoops. Before you know it, your personal billboard is on default mode and you are reaching for the same old accessories. Where is the fun in that? And where is that extra burst of empowerment you get from wearing something new and exciting that just makes you feel great? While your classics will never go out of style, if you wear them every day, you stop noticing them, and so does everybody else.

Celebrities are good role models when it comes to keeping their styles fresh and exciting. They have to be—for them, projecting a glamorous lifestyle is their job. Whether they are walking the red carpet, on a shopping spree, or at the beach, they are always using fashion to say something to the world. Their of-the-moment looks seem to effortlessly project confidence and make them feel desired, strong, and sexy.

Yet, the truth is, celebrities don't look that fabulous on their own. They have a slew of makeup artists, hairstylists, and clothing experts working together to create the looks we all love. And the resources these celebrities have are unbelievable. I recall meeting a well-known celebrity stylist to go over jewelry she needed for a famous client. I marveled at the vast quantities of clothing and shoes around her office. There were racks of designer clothing, bins of high-end shoes, and, of course, boxes and boxes of earrings. Can you imagine having these options at your fingertips? No wonder celebrities make a statement with every look.

In the ten years since Double Happiness Jewelry's founding, I have learned how celebrities and their stylists work. It has been a crazy, interesting journey, from the company's humble beginning in my garage to today's worldwide distribution at more than four hundred stores; monthly features in major magazines such as *Elle*, *In Style*, *Cosmopolitan*, *Vogue*, *Harper's Bazaar*, and *Lucky*; and, of course, happy celebrity clients, such as Oprah Winfrey, Jessica Simpson, Alicia Keys, Tyra Banks, Britney Spears, Rachael Ray, and Beyoncé, to name a few.

The Earring Style Book teaches you how to create the same earring designs that you have seen featured in fashion magazines and worn by your favorite celebrities, so that you can make your own fashion statement—no stylist required. Whether you're drawn to Everyday Chic or Rock and Roll, feel like a Bohemian Beauty or a Glamour Girl, you're sure to find the earrings to help you shout your message to the world. I think every woman has a bit of each style within her. I know I do. From the intricate Lourdes earrings to the elegantly simple Marra, *The Earring Style Book* offers you tons of DIY options that will revolutionize and revive any outfit.

HOW TO USE THIS BOOK

No matter what kind of woman you choose to be, you'll want to get started in Chapter 1 by learning about the basic materials and tools you'll need for every earring project in this book. The step-by-step technique instructions in Chapter 2 form the backbone of jewelry design and will have you ready to design your own star-worthy earring styles. Then, dive into the earring projects. If there are portions of a given design that are new to you, no problem—look at the list of techniques at the start of the project and refer to the basic technique instructions in Chapter 2. You will note that each design lists the techniques used, for easy reference to the techniques explained in this chapter. You'll also find a list of the materials and tools needed, how long each earring pair should take to make, the finished size of the earrings, and a prep-work section. If you organize

Life is full of choices, and every day is an opportunity to ask, "Who do I want to be today?"

your exact materials needed and do the prep work per earring as listed, then you will be left with exactly the right amount of materials needed to prep and make the second earring in the pair. The step-by-step instructions are for one earring only. I do this to keep your head and your work space clear. So easy. And once you finish the first earring, the second one will be that much simpler to make.

So read this book, feel inspired, pick a style or a mood, and run with it. Make yourself a pair of earrings that say something, and wear them when you face the world. It's fun and empowering—and when people come up to you and compliment your earrings (and I promise you, they will), smile politely, take in that positive energy, and say, "Thanks, I made them." It feels good, trust me.

Television host Rachael Ray wears the Osiris earrings (page 144) (this page). Singer Jessica Simpson (opposite) is frequently spotted wearing Double Happiness Jewelry.

The beauty of the Everyday Chic woman is classic and iconic. Like Jackie O and Audrey Hepburn, her style represents confidence and intelligence. Her clothing choices don't revolve around the trend of the week but rather reflect clean lines, elegance, and feminine charm. Whether she is at work, leading a PTA meeting, or just running around doing errands, she is always elegant and refined.

EVERYDAY CHIC

The earrings for this modern woman are often subtle, simple, and unembellished. They are no-brainer, go-with-everything earrings that lend a certain grace to any occasion. These earrings are my workweek go-to earrings. Turn to page 40 for these styles.

The Bohemian Beauty is radiant and ethereal, unstudied and unpredictable. In the 1960s, Talitha Getty epitomized this free-spirited type of glamour, encompassing the exoticism of the East with the hedonism of the West. Today, celebs like Sienna Miller and Nicole Richie reflect the enduring popularity of boho styles. The bohemian beauty is a bit of a flower child, gypsy, and traveler. She represents a nonconformist with an artistic eye. Her earrings and other jewelry are often large, embellished, and ethnic-inspired. She may be working at her own company, playing in the park with her children, or on her way to lunch with friends, but her look is always fresh, unique, and admired.

BOHEMIAN BEAUTY

The earrings that suit this inspired woman are usually bold and are perfect for casually updating any outfit. I often wear these earrings on weekends, when I am feeling light and free and just want to glide through my day. Turn to page 64 for these styles.

GLAMOUR GIRL

A Glamour Girl's beauty is bold, and it shines! When she walks into a room, all eyes are on her. Like Nicole Kidman standing tall on the red carpet, a Glamour Girl's style represents a woman who is confident, powerful, and comfortable in her own skin. She often shows a flair for dramatic makeup and clothes with sex appeal, and the Glamour Girl knows she stands out in a crowd—and she is not afraid of the attention. Whether working at the office, drinking cocktails with friends, or on her way to a party, she is striking, gorgeous, and exciting to be with.

Glamorous earrings are often dramatic and incorporate long, dangly chains; big bold hoops; and lots of stones and crystals into their designs. The Glamour Girl collection is shiny, bright, and sexy. I wear these earrings when I want to be noticed. Special dinners and nights out dancing are the perfect occasions to show off these earrings. Turn to page 102 for these styles.

A Rock and Roll woman is edgy, funky, and a bit rebellious, like Debbie Harry, Gwen Stefani, or Kate Moss. Her clothing might be ripped, studded, or worn tight or in layers, and her look helps bring her sexy attitude wherever she goes. She is captivating, provocative, and capricious, and her style represents a woman who is secure, is self-possessed, and likes excitement. Whether she is working on a new project, dancing to her favorite song, or just cooking dinner for her family, she is always distinctive, always fun, and always exceptional.

ROCK AND ROLL

Of course, earrings for a Rock and Roll woman must be cool, innovative, and cutting-edge. I wear these earrings when I want to feel modern, edgy, a bit tough, and oh-so-sexy. My recommendation? Create these earrings in combinations of black, red, and metallic—leather pants optional. Turn to page 130 for these styles.

Chapter 1

Fundamentally good jewelry design breaks down into four parts: beads, wire, tools, and the love story that takes place between you and these materials. Making beautiful jewelry is a lot like dating. First, you have to find something you like, something that pleases you. Then, you have to take the time to get to know it—does it listen to you? Can you hear what it is saying about what it wants to be? Like all good relationships, making jewelry takes time and energy.

MAKING FRIENDS WITH YOUR MATERIALS

In this chapter you will get to know your materials, exploring the types and characteristics of beads as well as the many different aspects of wire and how it can be used to make earrings. Finally, you will learn about a few fundamental jewelry-making tools—pliers, wire cutters, and mandrels—as well as some additional tools that will give you more freedom to design and make crafting easier.

Meticulous
on blend from
rt Allen: rob-
endesign.com:

Ralph Lauren $1195

GEMSTONES & OTHER BEADS

Gemstone beads are my love and the inspiration for all my earring designs. My obsession began long before I knew how to make jewelry. Maybe it was because all the colors and shapes and sparkly possibilities of gemstone beads reminded me of childhood. Walking among bins of colorful stones has always felt a bit like walking into a candy store, a feast for the senses as well as for the imagination. I still get a thrill when I pick out beads for a new project. My first favorite stone was turquoise, with its black striations cutting through the irregular blue-green hues. Then I fell in love with citrine. Its warm, golden nature made me think of summer evenings, when the night air is warm and soft. Now, I have too many "favorite" gemstones to count, and it seems that each time I learn about a new bead, the list grows by one more.

For me, working with beads is just plain fun. Although I prefer natural gemstone beads, beads can be made from anything. A bead could be an item you have found, one you have crafted out of wire or metal, or one you have bought in a store. As long as you think it's beautiful and you want to make jewelry out of it—go for it!

In this book I work with natural and synthetic gemstones and other man-made beads. Gemstones are finite in nature and can be seen truly as gifts from the earth. It is difficult to say what exactly transforms a rock or mineral into a gemstone—it really is in the eye of the beholder. This does not stop people from trying to categorize them, however, and most people are already familiar with the terms *semiprecious* and *precious*. But don't be too quick to judge a bead based on these designations. Quality can vary greatly within these categories, making a high-quality semiprecious stone more valuable than a low-quality precious stone, and vice versa. What I find special about semiprecious and precious beads is that they are unique. No two beads will *ever* be exactly the same. Therefore, prices of gemstone beads are not fixed and will fluctuate. When you consider which gemstone beads to buy, remember that a stone's formation is an organic process. It may take hundreds and thousands of years for a stone to form deep within the earth—or it can be made in as few as one to six weeks in a laboratory. Choosing the right beads for your earrings is a decision you'll want to make based on your own unique needs and preferences.

The Look of Natural Gemstones

Undoubtedly, the most important aspect of gemstone beads that most of us consider is the look of the stone. We are often first drawn to the color and then to the sparkle or opacity of a given bead. The type of cutting and polishing a stone undergoes helps bring forth its beauty. Transparent stones are often cut and then faceted to help the color emerge from the stone and maximize the light reflecting off the stone's surface and its refraction through the stone's interior, creating more of a sparkle effect. The crystal quartz used in the Marilyn earrings (page 42) exemplifies how faceting enriches a transparent stone. Almost all the beads used in this book are faceted. Opaque stones, such as turquoise, obsidian, and Botswana agate, are commonly cut into shapes and polished to show off the stones' surface colors and properties. The azurite stones used in the Britney earrings (page 138) illustrate how polishing brings out the beautiful color in an opaque, nonfaceted stone.

It is worth noting that the majority of natural gemstone beads today are cosmetically treated to enhance their colors, often through dyeing or heat treatment. In most cases, the enhancements are essentially permanent, and treated stones tend to age as do other gemstones, their colors becoming slightly more dull or faded with time. Careful cleaning and storage of all your gemstone jewelry will keep it looking its best (page 158).

Other Types of Beads

Although gemstones are now widely available in a range of prices and sizes, synthetic (man-made) beads are also great, typically lightweight, choices for earring design. Synthetic beads can be made out of metal, plastic, glass, or resin and may resemble gemstones—or may be created with a look all their own. Non-gemstone beads I use in this book include cubic zirconia, Swarovski crystal, and Czech crystal beads, as well as small metal faceted beads.

You may have heard of cubic zirconia and thought, *That's a fake diamond, right?* Well, yes and no. Cubic zirconia (aka CZ) does have a reputation as an affordable alternative to diamond, but science, technology, and popular demand have brought about an amazing variety of shapes and colors in the stone, perfectly suited for beading. Cubic zirconia beads are relatively affordable and easily found at bead stores or bead fairs in many different shapes, including teardrop briolette, coin, rectangle, and faceted rounds. Like other beads, the colors vary, from clear, light pink, light champagne, and jet (opaque) to olivine, bright orange, light purple, and dark purple (opaque).

BEGINNING WITH BEADS

My love story with materials usually starts with beads. Every two to three months a bead fair comes to my town, and shopping these fairs usually kick-starts my design ideas for each new season. I just love walking through the shows and looking at the tables filled with beads of all different colors, cuts, and drills from all over the world. To find out about bead fairs near you, visit www.gemfaire.com.

BEAD SHAPES & SIZES

Gemstones are mined all around the world, and the bulk of them end up in China and India for cutting, shaping, drilling, and polishing. Workers and artisans craft smooth rounds, faceted rondelles, chips, pebbles, nuggets, and myriad other shapes and textures in a seemingly endless parade of sizes, giving you lots of options when deciding which stones you want to use in your designs.

The majority of beads you work with will probably be either center-drilled (i.e., drilled lengthwise through the center of the bead) or top-drilled (i.e., drilled widthwise through the side of the bead).

When purchasing beads, pay attention to the size of the drilled hole. Some bead holes are really large, and as a result, the beads may not stay in place properly on the wire. However, it is possible to try to support the bead on the wire by placing smaller beads on its sides. On the other hand, some bead holes are really small and may work only with a wire gauge that is too small to support the structure of your design. If that is the case, either rework your design or find a new bead. Fire Mountain Gems and Beads has a great reference guide on its website that charts the maximum metal wire size you can use with specific bead hole sizes (Resources, page 159).

The following is an overview of the bead shapes, cuts, and drills used in this book. For in-depth information on different types of beads, check out one of the many reference books available. A fun and inexpensive alternative to learning from a book is to go online and study retail websites. That is how I learned. See my suggested list of Resources (page 159) to further explore the world of beads.

BRIOLETTE (FACETED TEARDROP OR FANCY PEAR) A teardrop- or pear-shaped pendant bead with facets. Nonfaceted teardrop-shaped beads may simply be called *drops*. This shape is most often top-drilled, with the bead hole drilled from left to right at the narrow neck of the bead.

COIN Looks like a coin! This bead can be either flat or puffed and is usually center-drilled, with the hole drilled lengthwise along the center of the bead.

DIAMOND (CORNER-DRILLED SQUARE) AND SQUARE Beads with equal sides, depending on the angles of each side. Diamond-shaped beads are often drilled diagonally from corner to corner; squares are typically center-drilled.

NUGGET A slightly rounded, irregularly shaped bead. No two nuggets are exactly the same. Nuggets are typically center-drilled.

ROUND A bead that is just that, round. It looks like a smooth ball. It is always center-drilled. These shapes can be either faceted (cut, with many planed surfaces) or nonfaceted (smooth).

RONDELLE An oval-shaped bead. Rondelles resemble rounds with a slightly squashed shape. These shapes can be either faceted or nonfaceted (smooth) and are typically center-drilled.

Bead Sizes

Precious gemstones are prized by their size and weight, and are valued in karats. But beads like the ones used in this book are usually measured in millimeters. The smaller the millimeter size, the smaller the bead. For example, in the Lourdes earrings (page 60) I use 5mm rondelles, about the size of sesame seeds. Compare that to the 10mm coin pearl used in the Casablanca earrings (page 70), about the size of a Cheerio, and you will get the picture. So for normal gemstone sizing, when the gemstones are roundish in nature, you will always be given the size in millimeters. Teardrop-shaped beads have two measurements: One is the width of the base of the bead, and the other is the length of the bead from top to bottom.

3mm   4mm

6mm   8mm   10mm

DESIGNING WITH GEMSTONES

SHAPE How do you plan on using the gemstone? Some shapes lend themselves better to earrings than others. For example, a briolette is a really adaptable shape for an earring. It can be used as a dangle at the bottom of an earring, as a drop in the center of an earring, or wrapped onto a frame (the wire infrastructure of many of the earrings in this book, page 28) with other briolettes to create an eclectic effect. I personally find square shapes difficult to use in earrings—but just because I find them challenging does not mean it cannot be done!

SIZE How large of an earring do you want? Do you plan to place all the beads together? Is your design balanced, or does one bead overwhelm the others?

WEIGHT How heavy is the stone? Heavy earrings tend to be uncomfortable to wear. If you plan on using only one gemstone bead, and it is a bit weighty, you might be able to get away with it. But if you plan on using additional stones in your design, I suggest rethinking the heavy gemstone. You may create an amazing pair of earrings, but if you can stand to wear them for only five minutes, is it really worth it?

DRILL HOLE How is the bead drilled? Pay attention to the direction of the drill hole; it will affect how the bead lies in the design. I certainly learned this lesson the hard way! I recently became so obsessed with the color of some druzy gemstone beads that I forgot to look at the direction that the beads had been drilled. I purchased a few hundred of these stones, took them to my workbench, and realized that my original design would simply not work. Because of the way they are drilled, the stones flop over to one side in my design, instead of hanging straight.

WIRE & FINDINGS

Wire is your friend, and as in all good relationships, you will need to invest some time in learning about it in order to really communicate. Wire comes in a variety of types, metals, and sizes. It can be bent, molded, and pounded into any shape you can imagine. You may already be familiar with some uses for wire in jewelry making, such as creating loops, eye pins, and other findings to attach beads and pieces of jewelry together. However, in this book you'll also learn how to create frames for your earring designs. These wire shapes are the main structures of Double Happiness earrings and allow for unique designs that go beyond just beading.

Types of Wire

When deciding which type of wire to use for an earring, you'll need to consider the kind of metal you like best. You'll find 14-karat gold wire, sterling silver wire, gold-filled wire, and even copper wire to be among the options. I am a gold girl, and I prefer to work with gold-filled. As the name suggests, gold-filled is not 100 percent gold. However, this type of wire looks like the real thing and can be trusted to not flake, chip, or turn color. The two types of gold-fill wire are 14/20, which contains 20 percent 14-karat gold, and 12/20, which contains 20 percent 12-karat gold. The less gold, the lower the price—but the color for both is the same.

Don't be afraid to play with other wire choices, though. Many people prefer silver jewelry, and you'll find projects in this book especially suited for this precious metal as well. Or you may find yourself drawn to the warmth of copper or the richness of 100 percent 14-karat gold. Of course, 14-karat gold wire can be pricey. If you want to use 14-karat gold, you would be wise to be very practiced in the earrings' design.

In fact, I strongly recommend that you first practice the techniques necessary for an earring design, no matter what type of wire you decide to use. Using craft wire to perfect a technique is a great low-cost solution to avoid making mistakes and wasting costly wire. It comes in the same gauges as other wire, but it is *much* less expensive than the other mediums—about 70 percent less. It is a bit softer than the other types of wire, but it looks and feels so much like them that you can practice with it to get a pretty good understanding of your design.

Wire Shapes and Sizes

The shape and size of wire can vary greatly, from round, square, or half-dome to hair-thin or very thick. All of the projects in this book require round wire, the most common and easiest to find. Wire is sized by its thickness. The most popular wire gauges range from 14-gauge to 26-gauge. The smaller the gauge number, the thicker the wire. So 14-gauge wire will be *much* thicker than 26-gauge. Different gauges serve different needs. Use the chart, opposite, to help guide you in choosing the appropriate gauge wire for your earring designs.

UNDERSTANDING TEMPER

Wire comes in a variety of tempers. By temper I mean the hardness and malleability of the wire and its ability to hold its shape and to bend fluidly.

DEAD-SOFT wire is the easiest to work with and is extremely malleable. I choose dead-soft wire when working with larger-gauge wires, like 14- and 16-gauge.

HALF-HARD wire is malleable and quite easy to bend and shape at all gauges. I use half-hard 26-, 24-, 22-, and 20-gauge when connecting beads and parts of earrings and half-hard 18-gauge for creating frames.

FULL-HARD (or hard) wire holds its shape firmly, but I find that its stiffness creates unnecessary stress on my hands. I do not use this type of wire to create earrings.

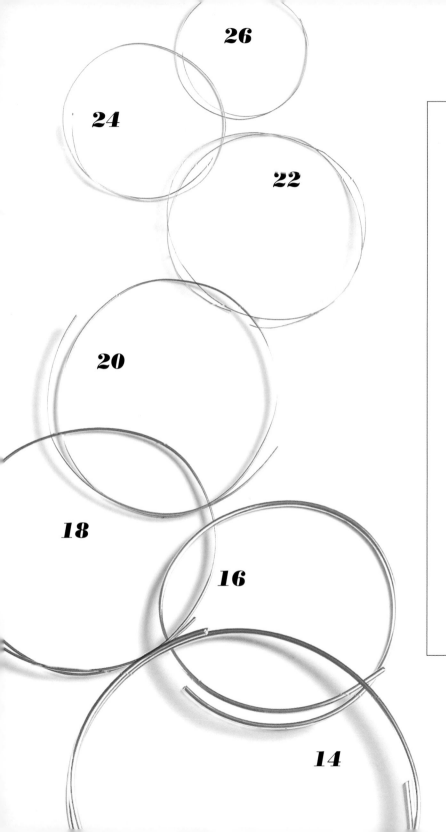

WIRE GAUGES AND USES

26 single and double wrapped loops, teardrop loop and wrap, wrapping single beads; attaching beads to frames

24 eye pins and head pins, single and double wrapped loop, teardrop loop and wrap, wrapping single beads; attaching beads to frames

22 eye pins and head pins, loops, teardrop loop and wrap; attaching beads to frames

20 ear wires, jump rings, eye pins and head pins; connecting frame pieces

18 frames

16 frames

14 frames

TIP: When you make earrings, I recommend that you prep all the wire you'll need in advance, so once you start the creative flow, you won't have to stop to cut wire or chain. It is how I organized the instructions for the projects in this book. This approach will keep your momentum up, and you may find that the earrings take less time to create.

If you are still learning about wire and its various gauges, I suggest fastening a clear piece of tape to each wire you cut and marking the tape with the gauge size. When storing your wire, simply place coils in resealable bags labeled by gauge.

Findings

I always thought the word findings was a strange word to describe jewelry components, the many parts and pieces people use to create and construct jewelry. The category "jewelry findings" encompasses literally thousands of items, including earring frames, ear wires, jump rings, clasps, eye pins, head pins, ring shanks, pin assemblies, tuxedo studs, and so much more.

Jewelry findings are easy to buy and come in a range of materials and price points. I suggest staying away from the less expensive findings, as they tend to break easily. At the other end of the spectrum are some amazing high-end findings that are intricate in design and may have gemstone accents, but they are often very expensive. When buying findings, you'll want to choose findings somewhere between these two extremes. If in doubt, ask someone at your local bead shop for assistance. (And learn how to make some of your own findings in Chapter 2!)

Dainty chain = 3mm

Simple chain = 4mm

Common chain = 4.5mm

Solid chain = 6mm

Rectangle chain = 7mm

JUMP RINGS AND CHAIN Ring-shaped pieces that connect parts of an earring together. You can buy premade jump rings for your earrings, but many people, including myself, like to make their own (page 39). At Double Happiness Jewelry, we find it is often easier to use chain instead of jump rings. This is because a piece of chain does not have a weak point—an opening. Instead, a solid ring of chain can be inserted onto a loop. The loop is then closed, and the solid link of chain provides a strong connection where an earring might need it most.

There are a myriad of chain options to choose from, so I've given each type of chain used in this book a descriptive name based on its size and shape. Use the guide on this page to help you purchase the appropriate chain for your projects.

When cutting chain for a project, one link will be lost in the cutting. Therefore, if an earring requires one three-link piece of chain, you will need to cut the length of chain at the fourth link. This fourth link will be cut in half, leaving three complete links.

You may or may not choose to use chain as jump rings. To substitute jump rings for chain in any instruction, simply refer to this page, which shows each type of chain with its corresponding dimension as well as popular jump ring sizes.

| 6mm | 5mm | 4.5mm | 4mm | 3mm | 1mm |

EYE PINS AND HEAD PINS Short lengths of wire with a loop or "stopper" at the end that prevents beads from just slipping off the wire. You can buy eye pins and head pins for your earrings, but you may like the freedom of making your own as well (page 38).

EAR WIRE The part of an earring that is attached to the ear. Types of ear-wire findings available include fishhook style, ear posts, ear clips, and—my favorite—leverbacks. Besides the difference in design, in my experience, each type of ear wire serves a different purpose. Most people buy their ear wires premade; just be sure to look for ear wires with precut rings on the bottom for easy attachment. However, fishhooks are quick and easy to make, as shown on page 39.

Leverback: a type of ear wire that creates a bit of a dangle effect and is good for light or heavy earrings. It works by connecting to itself in the back behind the ear, closing securely.

Ear Post: a type of ear wire that has two parts, an ear post and an ear nut. It keeps earrings close to the ear and prevents a lot of the dangle effect, making it an excellent choice for heavy earrings as well as light. As this ear wire reduces the motion of an earring, ear posts have the least amount of pull on pierced ears.

Ear Clip: a type of ear wire that is similar in concept to the leverback ear wire but uses a simple spring-and-pinch mechanism to clasp around the lobe.

Fishhook: a type of ear wire that creates a bit of a dangle effect and is best used only for light earrings. They can fall out of the ear easily if you leave them unsecured, so if you choose to use fishhooks, I suggest you attach an ear nut to the back to prevent the earrings from slipping out.

ATTACHING EAR WIRES

When purchasing ear wires, I suggest choosing those that have a precut ring at the base. This allows you to easily attach ear wires to your earrings. You can open and close the precut ring with pliers in the same manner as opening and closing a jump ring. Ear wires without a precut ring require a wrapped loop (page 33) to attach the earring to the ear wire. Don't take shortcuts and cut open an uncut ear-wire ring; the ring will often break. The project instructions in this book all use precut ear wires, which can be opened and closed at any time—they are so much more friendly to work with.

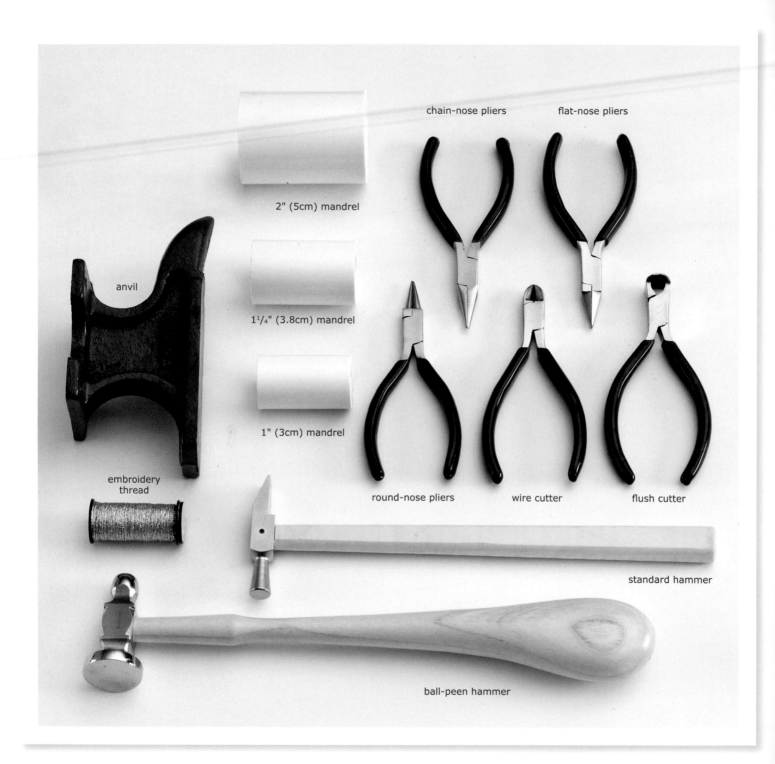

2" (5cm) mandrel

1¹/₄" (3.8cm) mandrel

1" (3cm) mandrel

anvil

embroidery
thread

chain-nose pliers

flat-nose pliers

round-nose pliers

wire cutter

flush cutter

standard hammer

ball-peen hammer

TOOLS

Like with any hobby or craft, certain tools are indispensable to jewelry making. I would be lost without my pliers and wire cutters, hammers and bench block, and mandrels of all sizes. You may even have some of what you need already in your home. Still, a little bit of research on which tools will best meet your needs makes a real impact on your finished projects.

To make the designs in this book you will need the following tools.

PLIERS The pliers you use for jewelry making should have smooth jaws that won't mar wire. I recommend three types of pliers for jewelry making: chain-nose, flat-nose, and round-nose.

Chain-Nose Pliers: my favorite kind. They have a narrow tip and are great to use in small places. I often use two pairs of these pliers—one in each hand—as I work, because these pliers seem to hold the wire better than my fingers do.

Flat-Nose Pliers: have a flat, squarelike head and need room to maneuver wire.

Round-Nose Pliers: have conical jaws. Your round-nose pliers will often serve as a mandrel for creating loops or jump rings, so it helps to have a pair with jaws graded from thick to thin to give you depth and options for size.

WIRE CUTTERS Because normal scissors are not strong enough to cut through wire, you'll need a special scissorlike tool called a *wire cutter*. A basic wire cutter will cut the wire with a pinched, angled edge. I also use a *flush cutter*, which has beveled diagonal jaws and leaves a "flush," or even, wire edge.

HAMMER I use two hammers: a *standard jewelry hammer* with a wide, flat saucerlike face for flaring my wire, and a *chasing hammer* with a round, ball-shaped face for texturing my wire. It is possible to get one hammer that has both heads, called a *ball-peen hammer*.

ANVIL OR BENCH BLOCK These tools are used as foundations for hammering. Materials used to make an anvil or bench block will differ, but I suggest using steel, as it won't mark or dent over time. Anvils and bench blocks vary in size and shape, from the traditional anvil shape to simple squares. I work with a bench block and place a piece of felt underneath it to absorb some of the noise as I hammer.

MANDRELS Mandrels are objects around which you wrap your wire to shape it. They come in a wide variety of sizes to create many items, such as jump rings and earring frames. Mandrels are measured by their diameter. You can use almost anything as a mandrel; in this book some tools used as a mandrel include round-nose pliers, a ballpoint pen, wooden dowels, and PVC pipe (¼", ½", 1", 1¼", 1½", and 2" [6mm, 13mm, 2.5cm, 3cm, 3.8cm, and 5cm]).

INSTANT GLUE AND EMBROIDERY THREAD Several projects in this book require the use of instant glue and embroidery thread. I work with Kreinik #16 embroidery thread, easily found online, and Super T adhesive. It is important to note which adhesives work with fabric and thread.

RULER For many projects, a simple 12-inch ruler will do.

In addition, you might find some of the following tools helpful.

BEAD REAMER A reamer is a round file small enough to fit into the hole of a bead. It is used to gently enlarge a hole that is too small for your wire.

FILE Files help you smooth wire ends that you cannot snip off.

KNITTING NEEDLE The length and consistent size of a knitting needle allow you to make a lot of jump rings at one time (page 39). The most common sizes I use are 4mm, 6mm, and 10mm.

Chapter 2

Wire is a fantastic medium to work with. It is soft enough to be shaped by hand but hard enough to keep its shape. Wire can serve as a foundation for earring designs as well as a connector, attaching frames together or attaching beads to frames.

EARRING TECHNIQUES

When I am working with wire, my eyes often wander to a quote I have pinned above my work space: "Jewelry is our personal link between earth and culture, metal and history, nature and art. It takes our form, it holds our marks, it truly interacts with our rhythms and cadences. In every era, in every land, in every culture, jewelry touched people. It still does."

I'm not sure whom to credit this quote to, but I love the ideas it expresses. I think about the phrase "interacts with . . . our cadences." That is what wire does. It holds our energy and our actions. It holds the twists we put it in; it holds the shapes we hammer; it holds our creations. In this chapter we will explore how to create with this most basic material, including how to make the four basic frames needed for the designs in this book. You will learn basic jewelry techniques, such as making simple loops and wraps and how to use wire to wrap beads and frames together. To close the chapter, you will learn how to make some of your own jewelry findings.

FRAMES

Frames form the backbones of the earring designs in this book. They provide the shape of the earring and support for the beads. I generally use 18-, 16-, and 14-gauge wire for my frames, as they provide a sturdier support than a thinner, higher-gauge wire. Frames can be left unto themselves, or embellished with stones, and even can be created free-form, by molding the wire with your hands, or in a more controlled way, with the use of mandrels. In the coming chapters, you'll find snapshots of the frames used for frame-based earring projects to help guide you as you work.

Frames can be as ornate or as simple as you like. But in my years with Double Happiness Jewelry, I have found a few frame shapes to be consistently popular, no matter what style of earring a person may be drawn to: the looped-back frame, the looped-ends horseshoe frame, the crossover loop-and-lock hoop frame, and the crossover loop-and-lock teardrop frame. As with any jewelry-making technique, I recommend that you practice making these frames with craft wire before using a more expensive material.

LOOPED-BACK FRAME A hoop-, teardrop-, or other-shaped frame that is open at the top, in which the two wire ends loop back, away from the front of the earring.

1 With wire cutters, cut a length of wire and place a mandrel at the wire's center. (Your length of wire and mandrel size will vary, depending on which project you are creating.) Bring both ends of the wire up around the mandrel. (a)

2 With round-nose pliers, create simple loops (page 32) on both ends of the wire. The loops should curve back, away from what will become the front of the earring. The tips of the loops should touch the main body of the wire frame. (b)

3 Place the frame, loop side up, on an anvil or bench block and use a hammer to gently pound the wire frame, flattening slightly, avoiding the loops. (c)

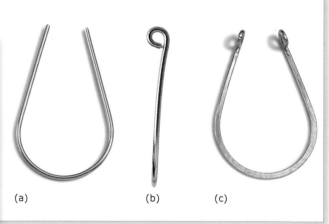

(a)   (b)   (c)

Used in: Christina, Halle, Ellen, Ali, Nicole, Solace

LOOPED-ENDS HORSESHOE FRAME A horseshoe-shaped frame, open at the top, in which the two wire ends are looped in opposite directions.

1   With wire cutters, cut a length of wire. (Your length of wire will vary, depending on which project you are creating.) With round-nose pliers, create simple loops (page 32) on both ends of the wire. The tips of the loops should touch the main body of the wire frame. (a)

2   Place a mandrel at the wire's center so that the looped ends curve away from the mandrel. (Your mandrel size will vary, depending on which project you are creating.) Bring both ends of the wire up around the mandrel to create a horseshoe shape. (b)

3   Place the frame on an anvil or bench block and use a hammer to gently pound the wire frame, including the loops. (c)

Used in: Vianca, Lourdes, Marra, Halle, Gisele, Nicole, Marrakesh, Shakira

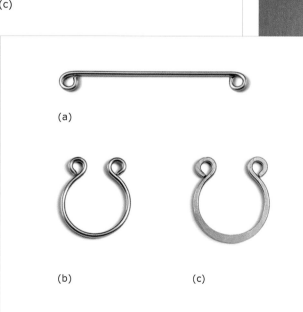

(a)

(b)   (c)

CROSSOVER LOOP-AND-LOCK HOOP FRAME

A round-shaped frame in which the two ends connect at the top, "locking" in place.

1   With wire cutters, cut a length of wire and place a mandrel at the wire's center. (Your length of wire and mandrel size will vary, depending on which project you are creating.) Wrap both ends of the wire completely around the mandrel to create a hoop shape. (a)

2   With round-nose pliers, create simple loops (page 32) on both ends of the wire. The loops should curve back, away from the front of the earring. The tips of the loops should touch the main body of the wire frame. (b)

3   Place the frame, loop side up, on an anvil or bench block and use a hammer to gently pound the wire frame, avoiding the loops. (c)

4   With chain-nose pliers, grasp the loop on the left side of the frame (make sure you are facing the front of the earring) and twist it 90 degrees upward, so that the left loop is now perpendicular to the hoop frame. (d)

5   With chain-nose pliers, gently open the right-side loop, creating a hook shape. (e)

6   With your nondominant hand, gently squeeze the frame together, hooking the top loop created in step 4 into the open loop created in step 5. With flat-nose pliers, gently close the right-side loop, locking the hoop frame. (f)

(a)   (b)   (c)   (d)   (e)   (f)

Used in: Rachael, Daisha, Rio, Priscilla

CROSSOVER LOOP-AND-LOCK TEARDROP FRAME

A teardrop-shaped frame (wide at the bottom, narrow at the top) in which the two ends connect at the top, "locking" in place.

1 With wire cutters, cut a length of wire and place a mandrel at the wire's center. (Your length of wire and mandrel size will vary, depending on which project you are creating.) Bring both ends of the wire up around the base of the mandrel, but *do not* bend the wire around it completely. Cross the ends slightly to create a teardrop shape. (a)

2 With round-nose pliers, create simple loops (page 32) on both ends of the wire. The loops should curve back, away from the front of the earring. The tips of the loops should touch the main body of the wire frame. (b)

3 Place the frame, loop side up, on an anvil or bench block and use a hammer to gently pound the wire frame, avoiding the loops. (c)

4 With chain-nose pliers, grasp the loop on the left side of the frame (make sure you are facing the front of the earring) and twist it 45 degrees outward, so that the left loop is now at a slight angle to the frame. (d)

5 With chain-nose pliers, gently open the right-side loop, creating a hook shape. (e)

6 With your nondominant hand, gently squeeze the frame together, hooking the top loop created in step 4 into the open loop created in step 5. With flat-nose pliers, gently close the right-side loop, locking the teardrop frame. (f)

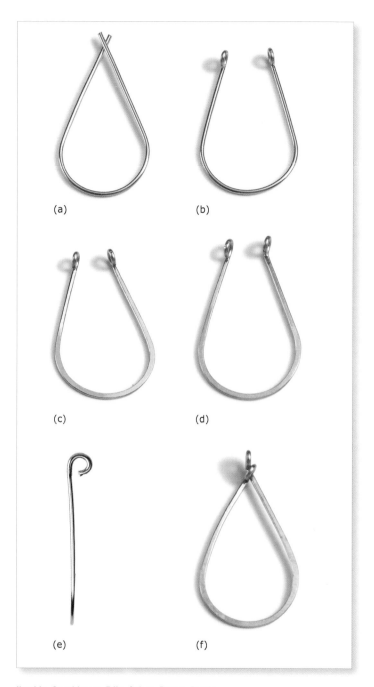

(a)   (b)

(c)   (d)

(e)   (f)

Used in: Casablanca, Edie, Salma, Reese, Fergie

DECORATIVE SURFACE TECHNIQUES

Creating a decorative surface on your wire can add a special touch to many earring designs. My favorite way to add texture and depth to wire is through pounding and chasing. The act of chasing—using a hammer or other indenting tools to sink the metal—leaves a textured surface on your design.

To chase, hold a wire or earring frame on an anvil or bench block with your nondominant hand and carefully pound the wire with a chasing hammer (or the round end of a ball-peen hammer). It helps to pay attention to how much you pound and where you pound, so your overall outcome is consistent and your wire is not overstressed.

Pounding wire and frames can also make them more durable. Very technically, this technique, called *work hardening*, creates movement in the wire's molecules. They begin to speed up and vibrate at a higher frequency. The end result is a firmer, harder wire.

I like to work-harden my wire with gentle pounding from a standard hammer, and you'll find that the projects in this book often call for this technique. You can also work-harden your wire by simply running it through your fingers or with subtle manipulation—for example, by twisting the wire of a jump ring from side to side. Be careful not to overdo the work-hardening, especially with jump rings, because overworked wire may weaken and break.

LOOPS

Loops are tough little structures that serve as *points of attachment*. We use simple, or open, loops when making frames to easily add chain, a jump ring, or some other finding to connect to an ear wire. Open loops also allow us to connect beads to frames and even to connect frames to one another. When used to create an eye pin, these loops are great for quick and easy connections with center-drilled stones, but stress on the loop may cause it to bend and the bead or frame to slip off.

To provide stronger and more decorative points or attachments, loops can be wrapped with wire at the base. Unlike an open simple loop, the only way a bead will slip off a closed wrapped loop is by cutting the loop. You'll learn how to make both single and double wrapped loops as well as the teardrop loop and wrap. These wrapped loops also permanently connect and attach bead dangles, allowing beads to delicately swing from frames, and from each other (opposite). All the wrapped loops build on one another in terms of difficulty, so they are easy to master. The trick with these techniques is to stay consistent. Remember how many times you wrap the wire around each closed loop so that your earrings will always match.

SIMPLE LOOP Loops are simply C or P shapes made by wrapping wire around the jaws of flat-nose or round-nose pliers to form an open circle—a loop.

1 Holding the pliers in your dominant hand, position the end of the wire between the jaws of the pliers. Run your finger over the tips of the pliers. You want to make sure that no wire extends beyond your pliers, as it will interfere with the shape of the loop. (a)

2 Rotate the pliers to bring the wire, ideally, to touch the wire tail. (b)

3 Using the pliers, adjust the loop if necessary so that the loop tip touches the wire tail. Be sure that when making adjustments, you grasp the loop at exactly the same spot between the jaws of the pliers. Otherwise, your loop may not be of even size.

To center a simple loop atop the wire tail:

1 Grasp the loop with chain-nose pliers in your dominant hand and the tail of the wire in your other hand.

2 Rotate or flick your wrist slightly to form an angle at the base of the loop. This will cause the loop to open up a bit. (c)

3 Insert the round-nose pliers back into the loop and gently bring the loop tip back to meet the tail-end of the wire. (d)

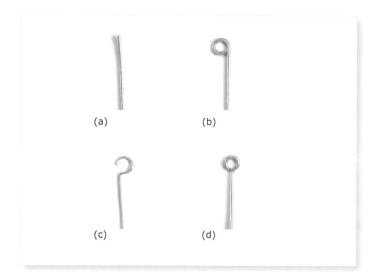

(a)   (b)

(c)   (d)

SINGLE WRAPPED LOOP Used as an eye pin (a bottom loop), to close an eye pin above a bead (a top loop), to create bead dangles and cluster drops, and to attach pieces of an earring together. It usually takes about 1"–2" (2.5cm–5cm) of wire for a single wrapped loop.

1 With round-nose pliers, grasp the wire ½" (13mm) from 1 end. Bring the shorter end of the wire around 1 jaw of the pliers, creating a simple loop, and center the loop atop the wire (Simple Loop, above). *Do not* trim the excess wire. (a)

2 Remove the round-nose pliers. With chain-nose pliers in your dominant hand, grasp the loop you just created. With your other hand, bring the excess wire around the long end of the wire. Wrap the wire around this long end 3 times, beginning at the base of the loop and working down the wire. (b)

3 With wire cutters, trim the excess wire from the short wire tail. (c)

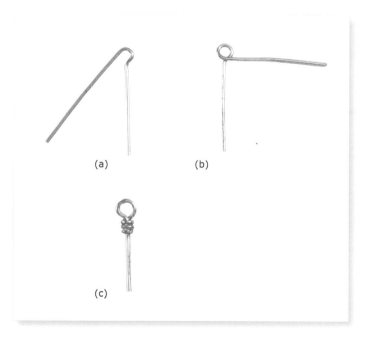

(a)   (b)

(c)

DOUBLE WRAPPED LOOP (WITH BEAD) The most common loop I use in my designs. It involves—you guessed it—two wrapped loops, one on each side of a bead. The double wrapped loop allows you to connect to other beads, pendants, or findings or to create chains of wrapped beads.

(a)   (b)

1   Create a single wrapped loop (page 33), and slide a bead onto the wire tail.

2   Just above the bead, create another single wrapped loop. (a, b)

3   When attaching double wrapped loops, insert the loop or finding to be attached onto the final loop just before you wrap it.

TEARDROP (TOP-DRILLED) LOOP AND WRAP Closely
related to the single and double wrapped loops and used
with teardrop-shaped and other top-drilled or pendant-
style beads. This technique involves forming a sort
of triangle on the top of the bead before wrapping. It
requires about 2" (5cm) of wire, depending on the size
of bead.

1   Slip the bead onto a length of wire so that ⅔ of the
    wire extends past 1 end of the bead. (This long end
    will create your looped closure.)

2   Fold both ends upward over the bead to cross each
    other. With chain-nose pliers in your nondominant
    hand, hold the crossed wires together. (a)

3   With a second pair of chain-nose pliers in your
    dominant hand, grasp the short end of the wire and
    begin to wrap this wire around the long wire. Wrap
    the wire 3 times and then trim excess wire from the
    short tail. (b)

4   With round-nose pliers, grasp the remaining wire
    right above the bead wrap. With your thumb, bend
    the wire tail over 1 side of the pliers, creating a half
    circle. (c)

5   Insert chain-nose pliers into the loop you have just
    created, and bend the loop back again to center it
    above the bead.

6   Insert round-nose pliers into the loop again and,
    with your thumb, continue to rotate the wire all the
    way to the tail to close the loop. (d)

7   Wrap the wire around the base of the loop 3 times.
    With wire cutters, trim the excess wire. (e)

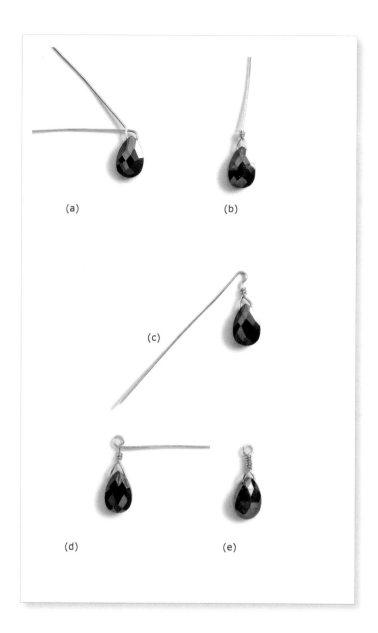

(a)   (b)

(c)

(d)   (e)

WRAPPING BEADS TO FRAMES

When I first began making earrings, wrapping beads to frames was a signature part of my designs. I was having fun exploring all the frame shapes I could make with wire and wanted to show them off—wrapping single beads and stacks of beads onto the frames as embellishments seemed perfect. There are many designs in this book that incw this technique, but the ones with the most "star power" are the Lourdes (page 60) and Osiris (page 144) earrings. The projects in this book all use either five or seven wraps—a strong design statement. For a different look, you may want to use more or less in your own designs.

WRAPPING SINGLE BEADS A technique for attaching beads to frames without using eye pins or loops.

1   Create a frame, and cut a length of wire appropriate for your chosen earring project. (a)

2   With your nondominant hand, hold the wire against the frame, creating a wire tail about ½" (13mm) long that extends beyond the frame toward your nondominant side. Using the longer end of the wire, press and wrap the wire against the frame 7 times, holding the ½" (13mm) tail to maintain tension while wrapping. *Do not trim the excess wire.* (b)

3   Either slip onto the wire the number of beads necessary to complete the design, or add them to your wire 1 by 1 as you go. Secure 1 bead against the frame with the index finger of your nondominant hand and, using your dominant hand, wrap the wire around the frame 7 times, securing the bead to the frame. (c)

4   Continue in this manner, wrapping 7 times after each bead, until all the beads have been secured to the frame. After adding the last bead, wrap the wire around the frame 7 times to secure. With wire cutters, trim the excess wire. (d)

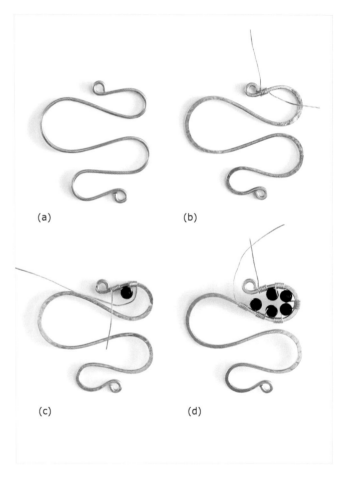

(a)   (b)

(c)   (d)

Note: I like my wraps to be neatly aligned with one another on my frame. If you find space between your wraps and don't want to unwrap and start all over, gently squeeze the wraps between the tips of chain-nose pliers.

WRAPPING STACKS OF BEADS Similar in concept to wrapping single beads—creating a frame and then wrapping beads to it—except the beads are wrapped in multiples, rather than single-bead vertical attachments. (This technique came about when I was trying to create the look of shattered glass. I never really got the shattered-glass look, but I was lucky enough to come up with what I call my "cup half-full" collection.)

1   Create a frame, and cut a length of wire appropriate for your chosen earring project.

2   Hold the wire against the frame in your nondominant hand; a tail-end about ½" (13mm) long should extend beyond the frame. Press and wrap the short tail of the wire against the frame 5 times, using about ¼" of wire. (The number of wraps between beads will vary, depending on which project you are creating.) *Do not trim the excess wire.* Hold on to this wire to maintain tension as you wrap.

3   Slip onto the wire the number of beads necessary to complete the 1st row of the design. Secure the beads against the frame with the index finger of your nondominant hand and, using your dominant hand, bend the wire toward the back of the earring and to the frame. Wrap the wire around the frame twice, and add a 2nd column of beads. (a)

4   Continue to add and wrap rows of beads to the frame in this manner to complete the design. Wrap the wire around the frame 5 times to secure. (b)

5   With wire cutters, trim the excess wire.

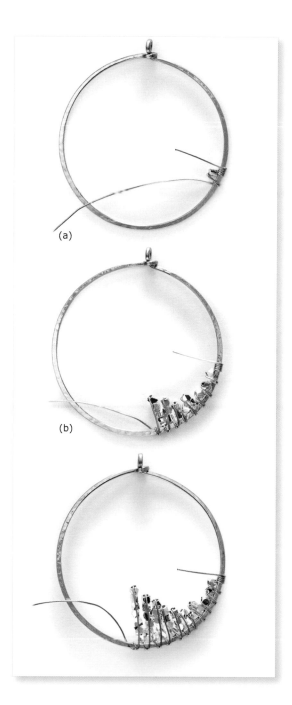

(a)

(b)

FINDINGS

You can buy findings at any craft or bead store. However, in this book, you will learn how exciting and unique your designs can be when you create your own findings. (All the earring frames in this book are technically considered findings, for example.)

This section teaches you how to make your own eye pins, jump rings, and ear wires, too. Do you know what that means? Your designs, and your creative expansion on the designs in this book, cannot be bought by others in stores! They are uniquely and totally yours! Maybe the word "finding" in jewelry design means that these are the parts and pieces you can create to help you "find" your own unique creative expression.

EYE PINS AND HEAD PINS Lengths of wire that allow you to incorporate beads into a jewelry design. I suggest using 20- to 24-gauge wire when making eye pins and head pins, as these gauges fit through most beads and are strong enough to withstand the normal pulling and twisting that comes with wear. You will need 1"–2" (2.5cm–5cm) of wire, on average, depending on the size of the bead.

1   With round-nose pliers in your dominant hand, grasp the end of the wire. Holding the wire tightly, use the pliers as a mandrel and rotate the pliers outward, away from your body, wrapping the wire around the jaw of the pliers to create a small simple loop (page 32). This loop should be larger than the hole of the bead you are going to put on the wire. (If the loop is too small, the bead will slip off the wire.) (a)

2   Remove the round-nose pliers and insert chain-nose pliers into the loop, and rotate or flick your wrist slightly to form an angle at the base of the loop back. This will cause the loop to open up a bit. (b)

3   To finish, re-insert the round-nose pliers into the loop and gently bend the loop tip back to meet the tail-end of the wire and close the loop. Hammer lightly to strengthen. (c)

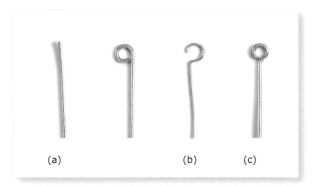

(a)   (b)   (c)

Note: To make a head pin, simply place the length of wire on an anvil or bench block. Hammer one end of the wire to flare it out. The diameter of the flare will need to be larger than the hole of the bead, so that it does not slip off the wire.

JUMP RINGS AND CHAIN Units of wire that allow you to connect pieces of an earring together, or incorporate beads into a design. To make a jump ring, simply wrap wire around a mandrel. The size of the jump ring will depend on the diameter of the mandrel. I use a knitting needle to make large jump rings (about 10mm), a ballpoint pen for medium-size jump rings (about 6mm), and round-nose pliers to create small jump rings (about 4mm). If you use round-nose pliers, be sure to wrap the wire in the *exact same* spot on the pliers for each jump ring to ensure consistency.

My favorite method for making multiple jump rings is to use knitting needles.

1 Wrap wire tightly around a knitting needle from top to bottom, creating a long spiral. The number of rings will equal the number of spirals on the needle, minus the first and the last (these will look like half-circles).

2 Slide the wrapped spiral off the needle. (a)

3 With wire cutters, cut each spiral in the middle to form a single jump ring. Repeat until all the spirals are cut. (b)

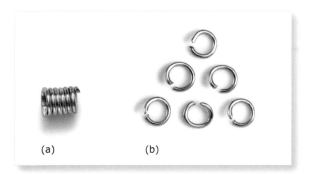

(a)   (b)

Note: To open or close a jump ring, I like to use two pairs of pliers, one to hold each side of the ring. I then twist the ring from side to side—never pull a ring open or push it closed. I like to make sure it is a flush fit, so I will gently slide the ring edges a tiny bit past where they meet a few times, to help the metal naturally align itself. You should feel it connect in your hands and may hear a click. Never open a jump ring any more than needed.

FISHHOOK EAR WIRES The easiest kind of ear wire to make yourself. I usually use 2" (5cm) of 20-gauge wire, which seems to give the perfect combination of strength, size, and length for my pierced ears. Using less than 2" (5cm) will put the earrings at risk of falling out of your pierced ears.

1 With round-nose pliers and 2" (5cm) of 20-gauge wire, create an eye pin (opposite). (a)

2 Place a pencil at 1/3 the length of the wire, measuring from the eye-pin loop. With your fingers, press the wire against the pencil, creating an arch. (b)

3 Place the ear wire on an anvil or bench block and use a hammer to gently pound the top of the arch, slightly flaring the wire.

4 Holding the ear wire in your nondominant hand, run the thumb of your dominant hand down the tail of the wire to create a slight curve about 1/3 of the way from the end of the wire. (c)

5 If necessary, use wire cutters and a file to trim and file the end of the wire to the desired length.

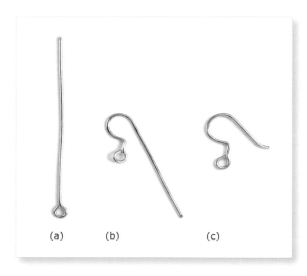

(a)   (b)   (c)

Chapter 3

Classic, perfectly at ease, beautiful. Everyday Chic earrings are your go-to earrings for effortless style. If you've never made earrings before, or if you need to whip up a pair of earrings in a flash, the designs in this chapter are a great place to start. Some designs take as little as as five minutes to make! In these projects you will practice the most basic

EVERYDAY CHIC

wire-wrapping techniques, such as the teardrop loop and wrap, wrapping beads to frames, and connecting frames. From the simple Marilyn earrings (page 42) to the more detailed Christina earrings (page 50), there is a design for any occasion. No matter your skill level or amount of free time, it's easy to be chic every day.

"If you've never made earrings before, or if you need to whip up a pair of earrings in a flash, the designs in this chapter are a great place to start."

faceted ...lles

MARILYN

This earring design is easy—easy to make and easy to wear. The Marilyn earrings are the kind of earrings that go with *everything*! This design dangles one beautiful bead at just the right length for women with both short and long hair. Plus, the close proximity of these earrings to your eyes will help to call attention to your face. Such simple elegance will take you from the boardroom to the playground, and from day to night, without a care.

time
5–10 minutes per pair

techniques
single wrapped loop (page 33)
eye pin (page 38)

tools
round-nose pliers
2 pairs of chain-nose pliers
wire cutters
ruler

materials
4" (10cm) of 20-gauge gold-filled wire
two 10mm faceted crystal quartz nugget
  beads
1 pair of gold-filled ear wires

finished size
1" x ½" (2.5cm x 13mm)

TO PREP *(for 1 earring)*

Cut one 2" (5cm) piece of 20-gauge wire.

TO MAKE

1 With round-nose pliers, create an eye pin from the 2" (5cm) piece of 20-gauge wire.

2 Slide a bead onto the eye pin, and finish by creating a single wrapped loop.

3 With wire cutters, trim the excess wire. With chain-nose pliers, attach the earring to an ear wire.

4 Repeat steps 1–3 to make the second earring.

weight watcher

Take care when choosing beads for Marilyn—and other earrings that prominently feature large stones. You may be tempted to reach for a stunner, but pay attention to the weight of that bead. It is never fun to wear earrings that are too heavy, but it can also damage a piercing. If your earrings hurt your ears, take them off.

If you love a bead (or an earring!), yet it feels heavy, you may try eliminating some of the drop and motion by using an ear post, which sits on the ear. Or you can transform that earring into a pendant by using a wrapped loop to create a bail (an arched or looped connector that allows you to attach your pendant to a chain or cord), and string that earring on a chain. You can make the second earring into a present for a friend, or alternate chain lengths and layer two necklaces for a style that is truly one-of-a-kind.

BETTY

The simplicity of this design—a subtle
hint of movement, and a bit of chain held
together by some gorgeous stones—makes
the Betty earrings perfect for all occasions.
The pendulum sway of the earrings brings
attention to the stones, to your eyes, and to
your body's movements. You are guaranteed
to feel a swing in your step when wearing
these earrings.

time
5–10 minutes per pair

technique
single wrapped loop (page 33)

tools
round-nose pliers
2 pairs of chain-nose pliers
wire cutters
ruler

materials
8" (20.5cm) of 22-gauge gold-filled wire
71 links (about 7" [18cm]) of gold-filled
* dainty chain*
six 10mm faceted blue chalcedony
* rondelles*
1 pair of gold-filled ear wires

finished size
2" x 1" (5cm x 2.5cm)

TO PREP *(for 1 earring)*

Cut one 4" (10cm) piece of 22-gauge wire.
Cut one 35-link piece of chain.

TO MAKE

1 To create a center bar support, begin a single wrapped loop at 1 end of the 4" (10cm) piece of 22-gauge wire, but *before closing the loop*, insert the end link of the chain onto the wire loop. Wrap to close. With wire cutters, trim the excess wire. (a)

2 Slide 3 beads onto the open end of the center bar support. (b)

3 To close the bar support, repeat the process used in step 1: Begin a single wrapped loop on the open end of the bar support, but *before closing the loop*, insert the other end link of chain onto the loop. Wrap to close. With wire cutters, trim the excess wire. (c)

4 With chain-nose pliers, attach an ear wire in the center of the chain at link 18.

5 Repeat steps 1–4 to make the second earring.

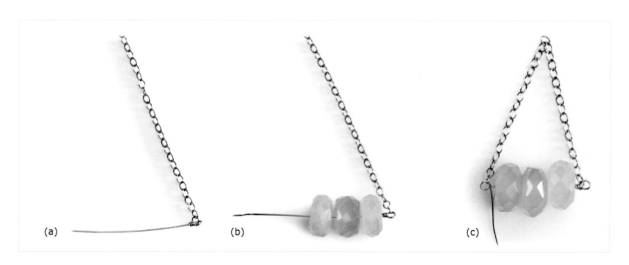

(a)   (b)   (c)

JUDY

This style is pretty, simple, and classic, just like its namesake, Judy Garland. Keep in mind that this earring has a lot of swing and may drop a bit farther from the ear than you are used to, so make sure to choose a bead with an appropriate scale and weight. A large, heavy bead can potentially cause damage to a piercing.

time
5–10 minutes per pair

technique
teardrop loop and wrap (page 35)

tools
round-nose pliers
2 pairs of chain-nose pliers
wire cutters
ruler

materials
4" (10cm) of 22-gauge gold-filled wire
11 links of gold-filled solid chain
two 4mm x 6mm light-gold cubic zirconia
*   briolettes*
1 pair of gold-filled ear wires

finished size
1¾" x ¾" (4.5cm x 2cm)

TO PREP *(for 1 earring)*

Cut one 2" (5cm) piece of 22-gauge wire
Cut one 5-link piece of chain.

TO MAKE

1   With the 2" (5cm) piece of 22-gauge wire, form a teardrop loop and wrap around a briolette. Begin the loop above the bead, but *before closing the loop*, insert 1 end of the chain onto the loop. Wrap to close. With wire cutters, trim the excess wire.

2   With chain-nose pliers, attach an ear wire to the other end of the chain.

3   Repeat steps 1–2 to make the second earring.

---

shape up

Judy's simple silhouette exemplifies one of the classic shapes for earrings — the stiletto. These simple earrings tend to be long and thin, just like the stiletto heel, and usually feature just one or two beads that hang directly from the ear wire or other finding. For more stiletto projects, check out Harlow (page 104) and Gwyneth (page 106). Drop earrings, such as Marilyn (page 42) and Marlene (page 48), are similar, though less exaggerated in design.

MARLENE

Part diamond-shape, part round, the Marlene
earring plays on angles and is one of the most
adaptable everyday looks you'll find. Switch
out the center and bottom stones, alter the
chain lengths—feel free to experiment with this
intriguing design. I used gorgeous amethyst beads,
but imagine incorporating large labradorite beads
to go from chic to fiery, or black onyx for a wild
night-out look. Have fun with this design, and
keep them guessing—never be predictable!

time

10–15 minutes per pair

techniques

single wrapped loop (page 33)
double wrapped loop (page 34)
teardrop loop and wrap (page 35)

tools

round-nose pliers
2 pairs of chain-nose pliers
wire cutters
ruler

materials

6" (15cm) of 22-gauge gold-filled wire
8" (20.5cm) of 24-gauge gold-filled wire
50 links of gold-filled common chain
two 10mm faceted amethyst coin beads
two 4mm x 4mm faceted amethyst diamond beads
two 2mm faceted amethyst round beads
1 pair of ear wires

finished size

1¾" x ¾" (4.5cm x 2cm)

TO PREP *(for 1 earring)*

Cut one 3" (7.5cm) piece of 22-gauge wire and two 2" (5cm) pieces of 24-gauge wire. Cut four 5-link pieces of chain.

TO MAKE

1   To create a center bar support, begin a single wrapped loop at 1 end of one 3" (7.5cm) piece of 22-gauge wire, but *before closing the loop*, insert the end links of 2 pieces of chain onto the loop. Wrap to close. With wire cutters, trim the excess wire.

2   Slide 1 coin bead onto the center bar support.

3   To close the bar support, repeat the process used in step 1: Begin a single wrapped loop on the open end of the bar support, but *before closing the loop*, insert the end links of the 2 other pieces of chain onto the loop. Wrap to close. With wire cutters, trim the excess wire.

4   With a 2" (5cm) piece of 24-gauge wire, form a teardrop loop and wrap around a diamond bead. Begin the loop above the bead, but *before closing the loop*, attach 1 end of chain from each side of the center bead. Wrap to close. With wire cutters, trim the excess wire.

5   Begin a double wrapped loop with a 2" (5cm) piece of 24-gauge wire, but *before closing the loop*, attach the 2 open ends of chain onto the loop. Wrap to close. With wire cutters, trim the excess wire. Slide a 2mm round bead onto the wire and create the final wrapped loop to close. With wire cutters, trim the excess wire.

6   With chain-nose pliers, attach an ear wire to the loop you just made.

7   Repeat steps 1–6 to make the second earring.

CHRISTINA

Long and elegant, the Christina earrings showcase
a diamond-shaped pearl in an unusual setting: a
free-form frame you can make in any shape you
like. This project shows you how to connect two
frames together using simple wire wraps, giving
you even more design options for creating your
own unique earrings.

time

30–40 minutes per pair

techniques

looped-back frame (page 28)
simple loop (page 32)

tools

round-nose pliers
chain-nose pliers
wire cutters
¾" (2cm) mandrel
standard and chasing hammers
  (or ball-peen hammer)
anvil
permanent marker
ruler

materials

6" (15cm) of 16-gauge gold-filled wire
8" (20.5cm) of 22-gauge gold-filled wire
44" (112cm) of 24-gauge gold-filled wire
6" (15cm) of 18-gauge gold-filled wire
5 links of common chain
two 4mm x 8mm flat white pearl diamond
  beads
1 pair of gold-filled ear wires

finished size

2¼" x ¾" (5.5cm x 2cm)

TO PREP *(for 1 earring)*

Cut one 3" (7.5cm) piece of 16-gauge wire,
  two 2" (5cm) pieces of 22-gauge wire,
  one 12" (30.5cm) piece of 24-gauge
  wire, two 3" (7.5cm) pieces of 24-gauge wire, and
  one 2" (5cm) piece of 24-gauge wire.
Cut one 3" (7.5cm) piece of 18-gauge wire and mark
  it at the center (1½" [3.8cm] from either end) with
  the permanent marker.
Cut one 2-link piece of chain.

TO MAKE

1   Create a round frame by wrapping the unmarked 3"
    piece of 16-gauge wire around the mandrel until the tail-
    ends of the wire meet.

    Create a looped-back frame in a V shape by placing
    chain-nose pliers at the 1½" mark of the 3" (7.5cm)
    piece of 18-gauge wire and push 1 end of the wire up
    against the jaws of the pliers. (a)

2   With round-nose pliers, make a simple loop on each end
    of the V-shaped frame, following step 2 of the looped-
    back frame technique.

    Place both frames on the anvil and lightly hammer, first
    with the standard hammer to flatten and then with the
    chasing hammer to lightly tap texture onto 1 side of both
    frames, being careful to avoid the loops on the V-shaped
    frame. (b)

3   Wrap one 3" (7.5cm) piece of 24-gauge wire over the cut edges of the round frame to hide them. Wrap lightly, so that the wire conceals the edges and joins the ends together but doesn't slip through the gap between them. With chain-nose pliers, pinch the wire tightly to the frame. With wire cutters, trim the excess wire. (c)

4   Wrap the other 3" (7.5cm) piece of 24-gauge wire on the opposite side of the round frame, directly across from the wrap created in step 3. With chain-nose pliers, pinch the wire tightly to the frame. With wire cutters, trim the excess wire.

5   With chain-nose pliers, hold one 12" (30.5cm) piece of 24-gauge wire centered vertically on top of the round frame so that the tail extends approximately 5½" (14cm) beyond the top and bottom of the frame.

6   With your fingers, wrap 1 tail of the wire 5 times around the frame, then bring it back to center on the back side of the frame. Wrap the tail 5 times in the other direction. Again, bring the tail back to center from behind the frame to wrap down the vertical wire 6 times.

7   Slide a bead onto the vertical wire. (d)

8   Repeat step 6 on the opposite side of the round frame with the remaining 5½" (14cm) tail, securing the vertical wire to the round frame. With wire cutters, trim all excess wire. (e)

9   With your fingers, wrap one 2" (5cm) piece of 22-gauge wire 4 times near the bend of the V-shaped frame. With chain-nose pliers, pinch the excess wire tightly to the frame. With wire cutters, trim the excess wire.

Christina earrings, back view.

10   With chain-nose pliers, gently open both loops on the V-shaped frame. Slide 1 link of the 2-link chain onto the side of the frame that is not wrapped. Take one 2" (5cm) piece of 22-gauge wire and create 4 wraps on the other side. With chain-nose pliers, pinch the excess wire tightly to the frame. With wire cutters, trim the excess wire.

11   With your fingers, wrap the 2" (5cm) piece of 24-gauge wire 4 times near one bottom loop of the V-shaped frame. (f)

Repeat on the other side. With chain-nose pliers, pinch the excess wire tightly to the frame. With wire cutters, trim the excess wire.

12   Hook the loops of the V-shaped frame onto the round frame on both sides of the top wraps. Close the loops. Attach an ear wire to the top link of the chain.

13   Repeat steps 1–12 to make the second earring.

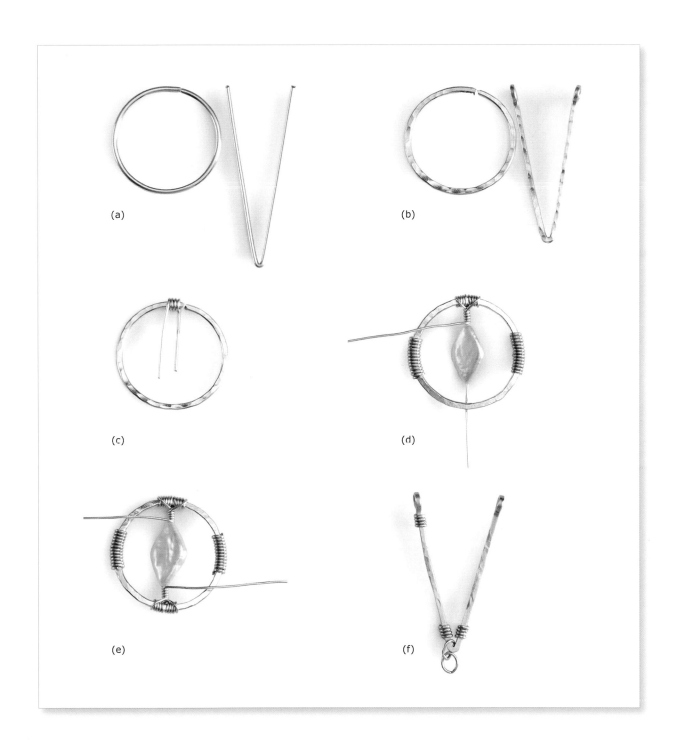

(a)

(b)

(c)

(d)

(e)

(f)

RACHAEL

These earrings define "all-occasion," from work to play. Case in point? Rachael Ray wore a pair to a book signing in New York City, and Beyoncé wore them on her tour of Ethiopia. Your travels may not take you downtown or to exotic locales, but no matter where you day ends up, you can be sure the Rachael earrings will have you looking *très chic*.

At first glance, these earrings may seem complicated. However, the design simply incorporates a double spiral wire shape with a crossover loop-and-lock hoop frame. In this project, you will learn how to create wire shapes and attach them to frames so that you can design and make earrings that are uniquely your own.

time

15–20 minutes per pair

technique

crossover loop-and-lock hoop frame
   (page 30)
simple loop (page 32)

tools

round-nose pliers
2 pairs of chain-nose pliers
wire cutters
1" (2.5cm) mandrel
ballpoint pen or similar-width mandrel
standard and chasing hammers
   (or ball-peen hammer)
anvil
ruler

materials

26½" (67cm) of 16-gauge gold-filled wire
3" (7.5cm) of 26-gauge gold-filled wire
3 links of common chain or two 4.5mm
   jump rings
1 pair of gold-filled ear wires

finished size

2" x 1¼" (5cm x 3cm)

TO PREP *(for 1 earring)*

Cut one 4½" (11.5cm) piece of 16-gauge
   wire, one 8¾" (22cm) piece of 16-gauge
   wire, and two 1½" (3.8cm) pieces of
   26-gauge wire.
Cut one 1-link piece of chain, if using.

TO MAKE

1   Create a crossover loop-and-lock hoop frame using the
    mandrel and a 4½" (11.5cm) piece of 16-gauge wire. Place
    the frame on the anvil and gently hammer to texture.

2   With round-nose pliers, create a simple loop at 1 end of an
    8¾" (22cm) piece of 16-gauge wire. Remove the round-
    nose pliers and grasp the loop flatly between the jaws
    of the chain-nose pliers. Using your fingers for leverage,
    rotate the chain-nose pliers away from you approximately
    4 times. The wire will roll 3½" times over itself, creating a
    spiral. (a)

3   At the other end of the 16-gauge wire, repeat step 2 to
    create another spiral, but looping in the opposite direction of
    the first spiral.

(a)

4   To create the arches between the spirals, place a ballpoint pen against the wire at the point where the swirl ends and the wire begins to straighten and, with your thumb, bend the wire over the pen to create a curve.

Repeat on the opposite side. The spiral shape should fit snugly within the hoop frame. Bend the arch as needed to ensure the fit. (b)

5   Place the spiral piece on the anvil and gently hammer to flatten and texture.

6   Fit the spiral shape inside the hoop. The spirals should line up evenly, 1 over the other at the top and bottom of the frame.

7   Wrap one 1½" (3.8cm) piece of 26-gauge wire 7 times where the center of one curve meets the frame. (c)

Repeat on the opposite side with the other 1½" (3.8cm) piece of 26-gauge wire, making sure to evenly line up the wraps. With chain-nose pliers, pinch the wire tightly to the frame. With wire cutters, trim all excess wire.

8   With chain-nose pliers, open the top loop of the hoop frame and insert 1 link of chain (or attach a jump ring). Close the loop and attach an ear wire to the common chain.

9   Repeat steps 1–8 to make the second earring.

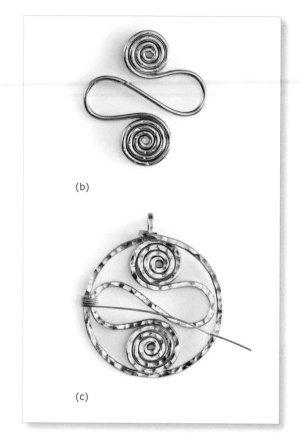

(b)

(c)

lost in a spiral

Don't fret if your spirals do not line up perfectly the first time. Think of your spirals as "in progress" until you actually wrap them to the frame. If one side of the double spiral is too short, the other side will be too long. Simply grasp the loop on the short side between your fingers, reinsert the round-nose pliers, and pull the wire toward the center. You will notice this action readjusts the other side of your loop, which was previously too long. Insert your pen into the arch and smooth the wire over the arch with your fingers to reshape it and ease out any angles that may have been created inadvertently.

VIANCA

Hoops have been the most popular earring shape for years at Double Happiness Jewelry, and the Vianca design is a classic that never fails to please. It's no wonder hoops are popular; they are said to be one of the first earring shapes ever worn. Where they originated in the Middle East as many as three thousand years ago, hoops communicated a lot about the wearer's identity. One look at a person's earrings, and the wearer's social status—whether religious, political, or tribal—was clear.

Today, earrings still send a message, and that's one reason Vianca earrings make the perfect choice for everyday wear. They are easy to adapt for any situation or style: Just use a different-sized mandrel to change the frame dimensions. I have made this earring in small, medium, large, and extra-large sizes for my sister, mother, best girlfriend, and me! This project has something for everyone.

time
30–40 minutes per pair

techniques
looped-ends horseshoe frame (page 29)
wrapping single beads (page 36)

tools
round-nose pliers
2 pairs of chain-nose pliers
wire cutters
¾" (2cm) mandrel
standard hammer
anvil
ruler

materials
10" (25.5cm) of 16-gauge gold-filled wire
72" (183cm) of 26-gauge gold-filled wire
23 links of gold-filled common chain
thirty-four 3mm faceted hessonite rondelles
1 pair of gold-filled ear wires

finished size
3¼" x 2" (8cm x 5cm)

TO PREP *(for 1 earring)*

Cut one 5" (12.5cm) piece of
   16-gauge wire and one 36" (91cm)
   piece of 26-gauge wire.
Cut one 11-link piece of chain.
Select 17 beads and organize from light to dark to create an
   ombré effect.

TO MAKE

1   Create a looped-ends horseshoe frame using the mandrel
    and the 5" (12.5cm) piece of 16-gauge wire.

2   With chain-nose pliers, hold the 36" (91cm) piece of
    26-gauge wire at a top loop of the frame. With your
    fingers, wrap the wire around the frame 7 times. Slide
    a bead onto the wire and secure it to the frame by
    wrapping the wire around the frame 7 times.

3   Continue adding beads, wrapping the wire around the
    frame 7 times after each bead, until you reach the end of
    the frame (about 17 beads total for each earring). With
    chain-nose pliers, pinch the excess wire tightly to the
    frame. With wire cutters, trim the excess wire.

4   With chain-nose pliers, open 1 end of the horseshoe
    frame and insert 1 end of a chain piece onto the loop
    and close.

    Repeat on the other side of the frame, inserting the
    other end of the chain onto the loop. Close loop.

5   Attach an ear wire to the center (6th) link on the chain.

6   Repeat steps 1–5 to make the second earring.

ombré-là-là

Vianca shows off one of my favorite color effects: ombré. A French word meaning "shaded," this term describes a color pattern with hues or tones that seem to melt into one another from light to dark. Designers like Diane von Furstenberg use this technique, and you can, too. Bead manufacturers often string multicolored gemstones in this way, like the hessonite rondelles used in the Vianca earrings shown here. Just remember to prep two sets of beads before you start to create your first earring so that the second earring will match.

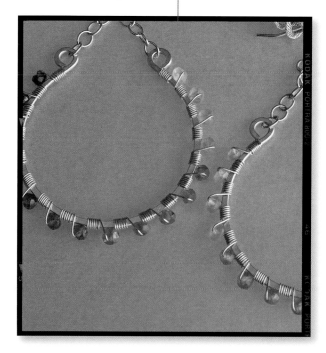

Note: If you would like your earrings to be mirror images, as shown, rather than matching, flip the second earring frame before attaching the ear wire. I prefer to wear my earrings with the light-colored beads near the face.

LOURDES

These dangling, layered hoops are a true Double Happiness Jewelry classic. The Lourdes earrings are a great example of how techniques build on one another. This two-layer look expands on the Vianca earrings. Just attach two horseshoe frames with jump rings to double the impact of the design. For your Lourdes, you may want to modify the size or number of hoops in the design, or mix and match beads. You can even take a cue from Vianca and arrange the beads to achieve an ombré effect. Bead manufacturers often string rondelles (used in this project) in this manner, making such a design quick to create.

time

50–60 minutes per pair

techniques

looped-ends horseshoe frame (page 29)
double wrapped loop (page 34)
teardrop loop and wrap (page 35)
wrapping single beads (page 36)

tools

round-nose pliers
2 pairs of chain-nose pliers
wire cutters
¾" (2cm) mandrel
¼" (6mm) mandrel
standard hammer
anvil
ruler

materials

14" (35.5cm) of 16-gauge gold-filled wire
12" (30.5cm) of 24-gauge gold-filled wire
9' (2.74m) of 26-gauge gold-filled wire
32 links of gold-filled common chain
7 links of gold-filled solid chain or four 6mm
  jump rings
fifty 5mm faceted turquoise rondelles
two 4mm x 6mm lapis briolettes
1 pair of gold-filled ear wires

finished size

3" x 1¾" (7.5cm x 4.5cm)

TO PREP *(for 1 earring)*

Cut one 2½" (6.5cm) piece of 16-gauge wire,
  one 4½" (11.5cm) piece of 16-gauge wire,
  two 3" (7.5cm) pieces of 24-gauge wire,
  one 18" (45.5cm) piece of 26-gauge wire,
  and one 36" (91cm) piece of 26-gauge wire.
Cut two 4-link pieces and one 5-link piece of common
  chain. Cut two 1-link pieces of solid chain (if using).

TO MAKE

1 Create a looped-ends horseshoe frame using the ¾"
   (2cm) mandrel and the 4½" (11.5cm) piece of 16-gauge
   wire. (This is the outer frame of the earring.)

2 Create a second looped-ends horseshoe frame using
   the ¼" (6mm) mandrel and the 2½" (6.5cm) piece of
   16-gauge wire. (This is the inner frame of the earring.)

3 With chain-nose pliers, hold the 36" (91cm) piece of
   26-gauge wire at a top loop of the larger frame. With
   your fingers, wrap the wire around the frame 7 times.
   Slide 1 rondelle onto the wire and wrap the wire to the
   frame 7 times.

4 Continue adding rondelles, wrapping single beads to the frame until you reach the end of the frame (about 16 beads), wrapping the wire 7 times after each bead. Finish and secure after the final bead by wrapping the wire 7 times around the frame. With chain-nose pliers, pinch the wire tightly to the frame. With wire cutters, trim the excess wire.

5 Repeat steps 4 and 5 for the smaller frame, using the 18" (45.5cm) piece of 26-gauge wire and wrapping the wire to the frame 6 times after each bead (about 8 beads total).

6 With chain-nose pliers, gently open the loops on the outer frame by twisting them to the side. Insert 1 link of solid chain (or attach a jump ring) onto each side loop. While the loops are still open, insert a 4-link piece of common chain onto each loop. Close the loops.

7 With chain-nose pliers, gently open the loops on the inner frame by twisting them to the side. Connect the links of chain on the inner frame to the loops of the outer frame, securing the frames together.

8 With a 3" (7.5cm) piece of 24-gauge wire, form a teardrop loop and wrap around a briolette. Begin the wrapped loop above the bead, but *before closing the loop*, insert 1 end of the 5-link piece of common chain into the loop. Wrap to close. With wire cutters, trim the excess wire.

9 Begin a double wrapped loop at the top of the earring with a 3" (7.5cm) piece of 24-gauge wire, but *before closing the loop*, insert the open ends of all 3 pieces of chain in this order: the 4-link chain from 1 side of the frame, the 5-link chain with briolette dangle, and the remaining 4-link chain. Wrap to close. With wire cutters, trim the excess wire. Then, slide a rondelle onto the wire and create a final wrapped loop to close. With wire cutters, trim the excess wire. With chain-nose pliers, attach an ear wire to the loop you just made.

10 Repeat steps 1–9 to make the second earring.

as seen on . . .

Some earrings just get a ton of press and celebrity support, and the Lourdes earring certainly leads the way. It's been photographed for many magazines, including Cosmopolitan, Marie Claire, and Brides, and has been worn by celebrities, such as country music star Trisha Yearwood and actress Brooke Burns. But the event that made Lourdes a Double Happiness legend happened on live TV.

I was at the office one afternoon when the phones starting ringing—everyone wanted to know if Oprah was wearing a pair of Double Happiness earrings on her show. I called my girlfriend, who records every single Oprah show, every single day, and ran over to her house. We sat down, turned on the TV, and . . . Oprah was wearing our earrings! The Lourdes earrings just so happened to be one of the first pairs of pierced earrings she had worn since getting her ears pierced! She is such a role model as a strong woman and humanitarian, I could not be more honored! (I am happy and grateful to note that she has gone on to wear a few more of our designs in the years since.) So make yourself a pair of Lourdes earrings and create a legend of your own!

The possibilities for these earrings are endless. Here, I arranged shades of green garnet in an ombré effect; the gradation of color ripples from light at one end of the frame to dark at the other.

Chapter 4

U npredictable, unique, flirty, and fun, the earrings in this chapter are for the woman who likes to play with her style, mix things up, and create a look all her own. In this chapter you will learn how to make some unusually shaped frames, such as the Casablanca

BOHEMIAN BEAUTY

(page 70)—a frame whose inspiration came from the sensual shapes of a Moroccan lamp. You will also learn how to organically wrap wire around a stone, how to make a hip version of a hoop earring, and how to mix and match techniques to create earrings for your mix-and-match wardrobe. From many choices for color play to new frame-making techniques, the options for creating bohemian beauty are endless!

"The earrings in this chapter are for the woman who likes to play with her style, mix things up, and create a look all her own."

RITA

I just love the way the chain drapes down to
surround the bead on these earrings. Because all
four lengths of chain attach independently, each
moves to its own rhythm with every step you take,
making this design free-spirited and sexy. Rita's
medium length doesn't scream for attention,
nor does it recede from view, which makes it perfect
for just about every shape of face. Feel free to
experiment with different shaped beads for the
center and sides as well as different chain
lengths to create an earring that is entirely
you and entirely original.

time

15–20 minutes per pair

techniques

single wrapped loop (page 33)
double wrapped loop (page 34)
eye pin (page 38)

tools

round-nose pliers
2 pairs of chain-nose pliers
wire cutters
ruler

materials

6" (15cm) of 22-gauge gold-filled wire
9" (23cm) of 26-gauge gold-filled wire
213 links of gold-filled dainty chain
two 4mm x 6mm olivine cubic zirconia briolettes
four 3mm pink tourmaline rondelles
two 3mm green tourmaline rondelles
1 pair of gold-filled ear wires

finished size

2¼" x ½" (8cm x 13mm)

TO PREP *(for 1 earring)*

Cut one 3" (7.5cm) piece of 22-gauge wire and three 1½" (3.8cm) pieces of 26-gauge wire.

Cut 1 piece each of chain 14, 20, 24, and 29 links long and two 7-link pieces of chain.

TO MAKE

1   Create an eye pin using one 1½" (3.8cm) piece of 26-gauge wire. Slide on a pink rondelle and use a single wrapped loop to close.

Repeat this step with a second 1½" (3.8cm) piece of wire and another pink rondelle to create 2 wrapped-loop dangles. With wire cutters, trim the excess wire.

2   Begin a double wrapped loop with another 1½" (3.8cm) piece of 26-gauge wire, but *before closing the loop,* insert the end links of the 7-link pieces of chain onto the wire loop. Wrap to close. Slide a green rondelle onto the wire and create the final wrapped loop to close. (This dangle will act as a bead link, connecting the ear wire to the earring). With wire cutters, trim the excess wire.

3   To create a center bar support, take the 3" (7.5cm) piece of 22-gauge wire and begin a single wrapped loop at 1 end, but *before closing the loop,* insert a pink bead dangle onto the loop. Wrap to close. With wire cutters, trim the excess wire.

4   Slide the bead-link dangle made in step 2 and then the ends of 4 pieces of chain onto the bar in the following chain-length order: 29, 24, 20, and 14 links. Slide a briolette onto the bar. Slide the opposite ends of the pieces of chain onto the bar in reverse link order: 14, 20, 24, 29, and bead link dangle, making sure that the chain dangle is not twisted.

5   To close the bar support, begin a single wrapped loop on the other end of the bar, but *before closing the loop,* insert a pink bead dangle onto the loop. Wrap to close. With wire cutters, trim the excess wire.

6   With chain-nose pliers, attach an ear wire to the top loop of the bead-link dangle.

7   Repeat steps 1–6 to make the second earring.

LAUREL

Give a nod to nature with this young, hip take on "going green." The brass leaf pendant bead, paired with gemstones, proves that staying in style can mean staying in touch with the earth. The design concept is simple: Two smaller beads descend down to a lightweight statement bead. If leaves aren't your thing, keep in mind that this earring design looks just as great with any two matching beads. Use beads from your own collection to make the perfect dangle for your Laurel earrings.

time
5–10 minutes per pair

techniques
single wrapped loop (page 33)
double wrapped loop (page 34)
teardrop loop and wrap (page 35)

tools
round-nose pliers
2 pairs of chain-nose pliers
wire cutters
ruler

materials
8" (20.5cm) of 22-gauge wire
four 10mm citrine coin beads
2 brass leaf or other pendant beads
1 pair of ear wires

finished size
5" x 1½" (12.5cm x 3.8cm)

TO PREP *(for 1 earring)*

Cut two 2" (5cm) pieces of 22-gauge wire.

TO MAKE

1 With one 2" (5cm) piece of 22-gauge wire, form a teardrop loop and wrap around a leaf bead, sliding a coin bead onto the open tail and closing with a wrapped loop. With wire cutters, trim the excess wire.

2 Begin a double-wrapped loop with the other 2" (5cm) piece of 22-gauge wire, but *before closing the loop*, insert this loop through the top loop created in step 1. Wrap to close. Slide a coin bead onto the wire and create the final wrapped loop to close. With wire cutters, trim the excess wire.

3 With chain-nose pliers, attach an ear wire to the wrapped loop.

4 Repeat steps 1–3 to make the second earring.

CASABLANCA

A few years ago I rented a movie called *Hideous Kinky* with Kate Winslet. It is a story about an English woman in the 1960s who travels to Morocco with her two little daughters in search of enlightenment and love. I became obsessed with this movie—the costuming, the scenery, and the energy all inspired what would become the Casablanca earrings.

Intended to represent the shape and allure of a Moroccan lamp, the Casablanca earrings evoke the bohemian and exotic. I made this version with a blue peacock coin pearl, but wrapping stacks of beads is another way to achieve a radiant, multicolor design. You can mix up the colors of beads you stack, making your Casablanca earrings look and feel as much like a Moroccan lamp as if you bought them at the Tangier bazaar!

time
15–20 minutes per pair

techniques
crossover loop-and-lock teardrop
   frame (page 31)
wrapping single beads (page 36)

tools
round-nose pliers
2 pairs of chain-nose pliers
wire cutters
standard hammer
anvil
¼" (6mm) mandrel
permanent marker
ruler

materials
13" (33cm) of 16-gauge sterling silver wire
6" (15cm) of 22-gauge sterling silver wire
two 10mm flat blue peacock pearl coin
   beads
four 2mm square faceted metal beads
3 links of sterling silver common chain or
   two 4.5mm jump rings
1 pair of sterling silver ear wires

finished size
2½" x 1" (7.5cm x 2.5cm)

TO PREP *(for 1 earring)*

Cut one 6½" (16.5cm) piece of 16-gauge
   wire and mark it at 2", 3", 3¼", 3½", and
   4½" (5cm, 7.5cm, 8cm, 9cm, and 11.5cm)
   with the permanent marker.
Cut one 3" (7.5cm) piece of 22-gauge wire.
Cut two 1-link pieces of chain, if using.

TO MAKE

1   With chain-nose pliers, grasp the 6½" (16.5cm) piece of
    16-gauge wire at the 3¼" (8cm) mark. Create a V shape
    by bending 1 end of the wire up against the jaws of
    the pliers.

2   Move the chain-nose pliers to the 3" (7.5cm) mark and
    bend the wire out to the side, away from the center of
    the frame.

    Repeat at the 3½" (9cm) mark, bending the wire in the
    opposite direction. (a)

(a)

3   Place the ¼" (6mm) mandrel against the top of the V shape and, with your fingers, wrap both ends of the wire around the mandrel. The ends of the wire will cross over each other, creating a circle. (b)

4   With chain-nose pliers, grasp the wire at the 2" (5cm) mark and bend the end of the wire to the side, away from the center of the frame.

Repeat at the 4½" (11.5cm) mark, bending the wire in the opposite direction. (c)

5   Bring both ends of the wire together at the top, crossing over each other, and complete the frame by using the crossover loop-and-lock teardrop frame technique, steps 2–6.

6   With chain-nose pliers, hold one 3" (7.5cm) piece of 22-gauge wire centered horizontally on top of the circular portion of the frame so that a tail approximately ½" (13mm) long extends beyond the sides of the frame. Wrap 1 tail of the wire 3 times around the frame. With wire cutters, trim the excess wire from the side wrapped to the frame.

7   Slide a 2mm square bead, a pearl coin, and another 2mm bead onto the wire. Wrap the tail-end of the wire to the opposite side of the frame 3 times to secure and close. With wire cutters, trim the excess wire. (d)

8   With chain-nose pliers, gently open the top loop of the frame by twisting the loop to the side. Insert 1 link of chain (or attach a jump ring). Close the loop. Attach an ear wire to the link of chain.

9   Repeat steps 1–8 to make the second earring.

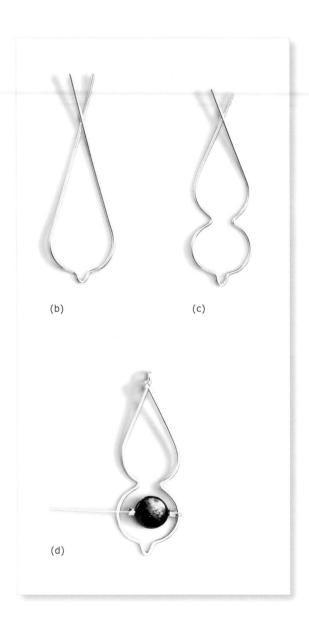

(b)   (c)

(d)

HALLE

What is it about a tabloid magazine that makes me want to spend $3.99 for pictures and gossip about other people's lives? Is it the beautiful people? Is it the drama? Is it the vicarious living? Honestly, for me it's all of the above. And I often think that the Halle earrings belong on those pages. It's an earring that will get you noticed. The bold, dramatic design is a true showstopper. People *will* want to talk with you about this earring, trust me. And wait till you experience the madness when you tell people you made it—the attention it creates may get out of control!

Okay, you may not find paparazzi hiding behind bushes to snap candid pics. And people may not follow you around to ask you for your autograph. But I do promise that when you wear the Halle earrings, you won't need to read about drama— you'll be creating your own!

time
30–40 minutes per pair

techniques
looped-back frame (page 28)
looped-ends horseshoe frame (page 29)
single wrapped loop (page 33)
double wrapped loop (page 34)
eye pin (page 38)
bead cluster drops (opposite)

tools
round-nose pliers
2 pairs of chain-nose pliers
wire cutters
permanent marker
¼" (6mm) mandrel
½" (13mm) mandrel
¾" (2cm) mandrel
ruler

materials
16" (40.5cm) of 16-gauge
sterling silver wire
48" (122cm) of 26-gauge
sterling silver wire
35 links of sterling silver common chain
twenty-four 3mm faceted apatite rondelles
1 pair of sterling silver ear wires

finished size
3½" x 1" (9cm x 2.5cm)

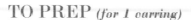

TO PREP *(for 1 earring)*

Cut one 2" (5cm) piece of 16-gauge wire,
   one 2½" (6.5cm) piece of 16-gauge
   wire, one 3½" (9cm) piece of 16-gauge
   wire, and twelve 2" (5cm) pieces of
   26-gauge wire.
Cut three 5-link pieces of chain.

TO MAKE

1 For the small frame, create a looped-back horseshoe frame using the ¼" (6mm) mandrel and the 2" (5cm) piece of 16-gauge wire.

2 For the medium-size frame, create a looped-back horseshoe frame using the ½" (13mm) mandrel and the 2½" (6.5cm) piece of 16-gauge wire.

3 For the large frame, create a looped-ends horseshoe frame using the ¾" (2cm) mandrel and the 3½" (9cm) piece of 16-gauge wire.

4 Create an eye pin from a 2" (5cm) piece of 26-gauge wire. Slide on a 3mm rondelle and create a single wrapped loop to close, making sure that the circumference of the loop is large enough to slide onto 16-gauge wire. With wire cutters, trim the excess wire.

   Repeat this step to create 10 wrapped-loop dangles.

5 Begin a double wrapped loop with another 2" (5cm) piece of 26-gauge wire, but *before closing the loop,* insert 3 bead dangles from step 4. Wrap to close, then slide a rondelle onto the wire. Begin the final wrapped loop, but *before closing the loop,* insert the center link of the 5-link chain onto the loop (at link 3). Wrap to close. With wire cutters, trim the excess wire. (This step creates a bead cluster drop for the earring.)

6   With chain-nose pliers, gently open the loops on the smallest frame. Insert 3 bead dangles from step 4 to hang from the bottom of the frame, but *do not* close the loops. (This frame will be the bottom portion of the earring.)

7   With chain-nose pliers, gently open the loops on the medium-size frame. Insert 1 bead dangle from step 4 to hang from the bottom of the frame. (This frame will be the middle portion of the earring.) Hook the small frame onto the medium-size frame. Close the loops on the small frame to secure it in place.

8   With chain-nose pliers, gently open the loops on the large frame. Insert the remaining 3 bead dangles from step 4 to hang from the bottom of the frame. (This frame will be the top portion of the earring.) Hook the medium-size frame onto the large frame. Close the loops on the medium-size frame to secure it in place.

9   On each open loop of the top frame, insert the end links of the bead cluster drop's chain. Insert the end links of 2 pieces of 5-link chain, 1 onto each loop. Close the loops.

10 Begin a double wrapped loop with another 2" (5cm) piece of 26-gauge wire, but *before closing the loop*, insert the end links of the 2 pieces of 5-link chain onto the loop. Wrap to close, then slide a rondelle onto the wire. Create the second wrapped loop to close. (This dangle will act as a bead link, connecting the ear wire to the earring.)

11 With chain-nose pliers, attach an ear wire to the top wrapped loop you just made. With wire cutters, trim the excess wire.

12 Repeat steps 1–11 to make the second earring.

bead cluster drops

By clustering your wrapped bead dangles together you can create fun, colorful, layered new looks. Start by making several double wrapped loop or eye pin bead dangles. Then begin another double wrapped loop, but before closing the first loop, insert your bead dangles into the loop. Wrap to close, then slide a bead onto the tail-end of the wire and finish the double wrapped loop. Ta-da! You've just created a bead cluster drop.

MARRA

The Marra earrings make me want to slip into a long, flowing skirt, pile on tons of bracelets, strap on high-heeled sandals, and fly to the Caribbean to go dancing. The frame and the chain create three layers of beads: the bottom teardrop bead, the bead dangles attached to the frame, and the center bead attached to the chain. I chose to make the sample all in bronze with just a touch of iridescence, so you can wear it with anything. Are you feeling Mediterranean? Play up the layers with different shades of blue. Thinking about Mexico? Try using green, white, and red. Any way you make Marra, you will feel bohemian and beautiful!

time
30–45 minutes per pair

techniques
looped-ends horseshoe frame (page 29)
single wrapped loop (page 33)
double wrapped loop (page 34)
teardrop loop and wrap (page 35)
eye pin (page 38)

tools
round-nose pliers
2 pairs of chain-nose pliers
wire cutters
1" (2.5cm) mandrel
standard hammer
anvil
ruler

materials
7" (18cm) of 16-gauge gold-filled wire
28" (91cm) of 24-gauge gold-filled wire
30 links of gold filled common chain
sixteen 4mm faceted fire polished bronze
  crystal round beads
two 8mm faceted fire polished bronze crystal
  round beads
two 4mm x 8mm fire polished bronze crystal
  briolettes
1 pair of gold-filled ear wires

finished size
3¼" x 1" (8cm x 2.5cm)

TO PREP *(for 1 earring)*

Cut one 3½" (9cm) piece of 16-gauge wire,
   eight 1½" (3.8cm) pieces of 24-gauge wire, and one 2"
   (5cm) piece of 24-gauge wire.
Cut two 4-link pieces and one 5-link piece of chain.

TO MAKE

1   Create an eye pin from one 1½" (3.8cm) piece of
   24-gauge wire. Slide on a 4mm bead and use a
   single wrapped loop to close, making sure that the
   circumference of the loop is large enough to slide onto
   16-gauge wire. With wire cutters, trim the excess wire.

   Repeat this step to create 6 wrapped-loop dangles
   in total.

2   Begin a double wrapped loop with another 1½" (3.8cm)
   piece of 24-gauge wire, but *before closing the loop*,
   insert the end links of 2 pieces of 4-link chain onto the
   loop. Wrap to close. Slide a 4mm bead onto the wire
   and create another wrapped loop. With wire cutters,
   trim the excess wire. (This dangle will act as a bead
   link, connecting the ear wire to the earring.)

3   With a 2" (5cm) piece of 24-gauge wire, form a teardrop loop and wrap around a briolette so that 1 side of the wire extends about ¾" (2cm). Wrap to close on this side, leaving a tail about 1¼" (3cm) long. Slide a 4mm bead onto the open tail and close with a wrapped loop. Wrap to close, making sure that the circumference of the loop is large enough to slide onto 16-gauge wire.

4   Create an eye pin from the remaining 1½" (3.8cm) piece of 24-gauge wire. Slide on an 8mm round bead and begin a single wrapped loop, but *before closing the loop*, insert the center link of the 5-link piece of chain (at link 3) onto the loop. Wrap to close. (This creates the chain dangle for the earring.)

5   Create a looped-ends horseshoe frame using the mandrel and the 3½" (9cm) piece of 16-gauge wire.

6   With chain-nose pliers, open 1 loop of the frame. Attach the bead dangles from steps 1 and 3 in the following order: three 4mm dangles, 1 briolette dangle, and three 4mm dangles. (These dangles should hang from the bottom of the frame.)

7   Insert 1 end of the chain dangle created in step 4 and 1 end of the bead link created in step 2 onto the loop. Close the loop.

8   With chain-nose pliers, open the loop on the other side of the frame. Insert the open ends of the chain dangle and the bead link. Be sure that the 5-link chain dangle is not twisted, then close the loop.

9   Attach an ear wire to the top wrapped loop of the bead link and, with wire cutters, trim the excess wire.

10 Repeat steps 1–9 to make the second earring.

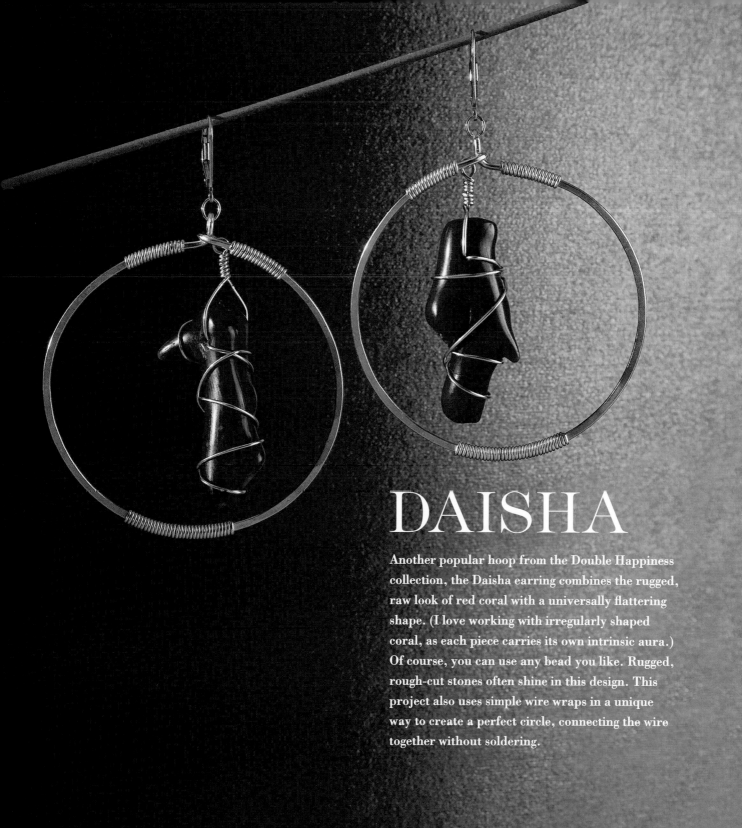

DAISHA

Another popular hoop from the Double Happiness collection, the Daisha earring combines the rugged, raw look of red coral with a universally flattering shape. (I love working with irregularly shaped coral, as each piece carries its own intrinsic aura.) Of course, you can use any bead you like. Rugged, rough-cut stones often shine in this design. This project also uses simple wire wraps in a unique way to create a perfect circle, connecting the wire together without soldering.

time

15–20 minutes per pair

techniques

crossover loop-and-lock hoop frame
   (page 30)
teardrop loop and wrap (page 35)

tools

round-nose pliers
2 pairs of chain-nose pliers
wire cutters
1¼" (3cm) mandrel
standard hammer
anvil
permanent marker
ruler

materials

15" (38cm) of 16-gauge gold-filled wire
56" (142cm) of 22-gauge gold-filled wire
2 red coral branch beads or other irregularly
   shaped beads
3 links of gold-filled simple chain or two
   4mm jump rings
1 pair of gold-filled ear wires

finished size

2½" x 2½" (9cm x 6.5cm)

TO PREP *(for 1 earring)*

Cut one 7½" (19cm) piece of 16-gauge wire, one 12" (30.5cm) piece of 22-gauge wire, and two 4" (10cm) pieces of 22-gauge wire.

Cut one 8" (20.5cm) piece of 22-gauge wire and mark it at the center using the permanent marker.

Cut 1 link of chain, if using.

TO MAKE

1 Create a crossover loop-and-lock hoop frame using the mandrel and the 7½" (19cm) piece of 16-gauge wire.

2 Insert the 12" (30.5cm) piece of 22-gauge wire through the hole in the coral bead, leaving a 1" (2.5cm) tail sticking upward. (a)

3 With your fingers, wrap the long tail of wire around the bead 3 times in free-form fashion, moving toward the bottom of the bead. Wrap the wire around the bead 3 times going upward, crossing the wire up and over the other wire wraps. Insert the long wire end back through the hole, opposite the other tail-end. (b)

4 Close with a teardrop loop and wrap, using 5 wraps to add bulk and strength to the closure. (c)

5 Hold the 8" (20.5cm) piece of 22-gauge wire against the frame, aligning the bottom center of the frame with the marked center of the wire. Begin to wrap 1 end of the wire around the frame, away from center. With chain-nose pliers, pinch the wire tightly to the frame.

   Repeat with the other end of the wire, wrapping in the opposite direction. With wire cutters, trim the excess wire.

6   Take a 4" (10cm) piece of 22-gauge wire and place 1 end next to a loop at the top of the frame. Wrap the length of the wire around the frame, away from the loop. With chain-nose pliers, pinch the wire tightly to the frame.

     Repeat with a second 4" (10cm) piece of wire, beginning at the opposite loop, wrapping in the opposite direction. With wire cutters, trim the excess wire.

7   With chain-nose pliers, gently open the bottom side loop, making sure to keep the lock in place. Insert the wrapped coral bead dangle. Close the loop.

8   With chain-nose pliers, gently open the lock and insert 1 link of chain (or attach a jump ring). Close the lock. Attach an ear wire to the chain link.

9   Repeat steps 1–8 to make the second earring.

wrapping beads with wire

Wrapping wire around a bead in free-form fashion doesn't just enhance the bead's beauty, it also protects the bead. Coral beads, for example, tend to be fragile and chip easily. I wanted a way to protect the bead without compromising design. By wrapping the bead with wire, I provide stability as well as protection, should the earrings fall or bang against a hard surface. When considering whether to wrap a bead in this manner, ensure that the hole in the bead is large enough for the wire to go through it twice. You may need to adjust the wire gauge you use to wrap the bead if the drilled hole is too small.

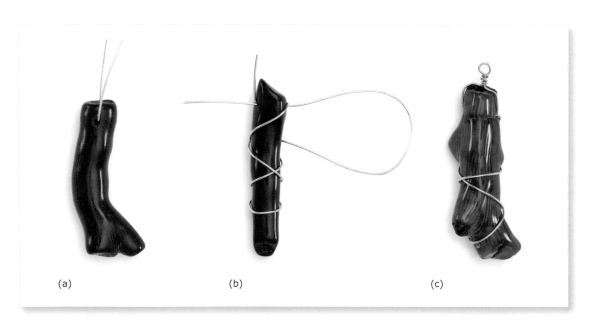

(a)   (b)   (c)

MARRAKESH

Historians believe that earrings were first worn as amulets to ward off evil spirits, so protect yourself and those you love! Make yourself and everyone you know a pair of Marrakesh earrings. This design is inspired by ancient traditions and antiquities, using chain, bead dangles, and a chandelier shape to bring to mind steamy *souks* and carefree travel. With earrings so gorgeous and exotic, there is no way any evil spirit will be able to invade your space!

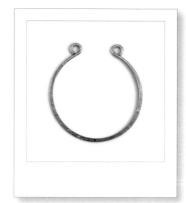

time

30–45 minutes per pair

techniques

looped-ends horseshoe frame (page 29)
single wrapped loop (page 33)
double wrapped loop (page 34)
eye pin (page 38)
bead cluster drops (page 75)

tools

round-nose pliers
2 pairs of chain-nose pliers
wire cutters
standard hammer
anvil
¾" (2cm) mandrel
ruler

materials

9" (23cm) of 16-gauge gold-filled wire
18" (45.5cm) of 22-gauge gold-filled wire
5½' (1.7m) of 24-gauge gold-filled wire
eight 8mm ruby chalcedony faceted round
  beads
twenty-six 3mm white pearl round beads
64 links of dainty chain
19 links of common chain
2 bar links of bar link chain or 1" (2.5cm) of
  any chain
1 pair of ear wires

finished size

3½" x 2¼" (9cm x 5.5cm)

Note: Using different kinds of chain is a fun way to personalize any earring design. I used bar link chain, found at most jewelry suppliers, to dangle my center cluster drop, but feel free to experiment with any kind of chain you like. Maintain design integrity by substituting chain of approximately the same length.

TO PREP *(for 1 earring)*

Cut one 4½" (11.5cm) piece of 16-gauge wire, three 3" (7.5cm) pieces of 22-gauge wire, and seventeen 2" (5cm) pieces of 24-gauge wire.

Cut two 15-link pieces of dainty chain, two 4-link pieces of common chain, and 1 link of bar link chain, if using, or ½" (13mm) of chain..

TO MAKE

1 Create a looped-ends horseshoe frame using the ¾" (2cm) mandrel and the 4½" (11.5cm) piece of 16-gauge wire.

2 Create an eye pin from one 2" (5cm) piece of 24-gauge wire. Slide on a 3mm bead and close with a single wrapped loop. Repeat 11 times to form 12 bead dangles in total.

3 Begin a double wrapped loop with another 2" (5cm) piece of 24-gauge wire, but *before closing the loop*, insert 3 bead dangles created in step 2. Wrap to close. Slide on an 8mm bead and make the final loop but do not wrap closed. Repeat 3 times to create 4 bead cluster drops in total.

4 Begin a single wrapped loop at 1 end of a 3" (7.5cm) piece of 22-gauge wire, but *before closing the loop*, insert 1 end of a 15-link piece of dainty chain. Wrap to close, but *do not* trim the excess wire.

5 Begin a single wrapped loop with another 3" (7.5cm) piece of 22-gauge wire, but *before closing the loop*, insert the other end of the 15-link piece of dainty chain used in step 4 and insert 1 end link of the remaining 15-link piece of chain. Wrap to close, but *do not* trim the excess wire.

6 Begin a single wrapped loop with the remaining 3" (7.5cm) piece of 22-gauge wire, but *before closing the loop*, insert the other end of the 15-link piece of dainty chain used in step 5. Wrap to close, but *do not* trim the excess wire.

7 Place the wrapped loop created in step 4 at the left center of the frame. Wrap the long tail-end of the wire around the frame 4 times, positioning the loop along the outside edge of the frame. With wire cutters, trim the excess wire. With chain-nose pliers, pinch the wire tightly to the frame.

8 Repeat step 7, but place the wrapped loop created in step 5 at the bottom center of the frame, making sure that the chain connecting the wrapped loops isn't twisted.

9 Repeat step 7, but center the wrapped loop created in step 6 on the right side of the frame, directly opposite the attachment made in step 7, again making sure that the chain connecting the wrapped loops isn't twisted.

10 Insert a cluster drop onto the first wrapped loop you've wrapped to the frame. Wrap the loop closed. Repeat with 2 more cluster drops, attaching 1 to the middle wrapped loop and 1 to the wrapped loop on the other side.

11 Insert the link of bar link chain (or length of chain) onto the open loop of the remaining cluster drop. Wrap the loop closed.

12 With chain-nose pliers, gently open both loops on the frame by twisting them to the side. Insert 1 end of each 4-link piece of common chain onto each loop. Close the loops.

13 Begin a double wrapped loop with a 2" (5cm) piece of 24-gauge wire, but *before closing the loop*, insert 1 end of a chain piece connected to the frame, the link of chain with the bead cluster dangle, and the remaining chain piece connected to the frame. Wrap to close. Slide on a pearl and make the final wrapped loop. With wire cutters, trim the excess wire. With chain-nose pliers, attach an ear wire to the top wrapped loop.

14 Repeat steps 1–13 to make the second earring.

SPF for stones

Staying out of the sun isn't just good advice for your skin. Your gemstones need some sun protection, too! Most stones today are treated and enhanced in some manner, and too much exposure to the sun will cause their colors to fade. Keep this in mind if your worktable is next to a windowts in opaque plastic bins as far away as possible from the window to avoid any damage the sun may cause. Of course, you'll want to shield your finished earrings from sunlight when storing them as well.

ELLEN

These are boho beauty at its finest. The teardrop-shaped frame encases three gorgeous, organically shaped spirals and incorporates emerald beads to recall the color of green grass, perfect for pairing with a flowing maxi dress—just like Jessica Simpson did on a trip to New York City. The spirals are made separately, then wrapped to the frame. I used a three-part spiral design in this project, but you may want to experiment on your own and create something totally unique!

time
50–60 minutes per pair

techniques
looped-back frame (page 28)
simple loop (page 32)
wrapping single beads (page 36)

tools
round-nose pliers
2 pairs of chain-nose pliers
wire cutters
¾" (2cm) mandrel
standard hammer
anvil
ruler

materials
12" (30.5cm) of 16-gauge sterling silver wire
30" (76cm) of 18-gauge sterling silver wire
6" (15cm) of 22-gauge sterling silver wire
60" (152.5cm) of 26-gauge sterling silver wire
3 links of sterling silver solid chain or two 6mm
  jump rings
twenty-two 3–4mm faceted emerald rondelles
1 pair of sterling silver ear wires

finished size
2¼" x 1¾" (7.5cm x 4.5cm)

TO PREP *(for 1 earring)*

Cut one 6" (15cm) piece of 16-gauge wire,
  one 4½" (11.5cm) piece of 18-gauge
  wire, one 5" (12.5cm) piece of
  18-gauge wire, one 5½" (14cm) piece
  of 18-gauge wire, one 3" (7.5cm) piece of
  22-gauge wire, and one 30" (76cm) piece
  of 26-gauge wire.
Cut 1 link of chain, if using.

TO MAKE

1   Create a looped-back frame in a teardrop shape using
    the ¾" (2cm) mandrel and the 6" (15cm) piece of
    16-gauge wire.

2   Using the tip of your round-nose pliers, create a
    simple loop on 1 end of the 5" (12.5cm) piece of
    18-gauge wire. With chain-nose pliers, grasp the loop
    flat between its jaws. Using your fingers for leverage,
    rotate the chain-nose pliers approximately 5 times
    away from you to create a spiral shape.

3   Place the spiral shape on the anvil and lightly hammer
    only the spiral to flare the wire. Flip the spiral shape so
    that the spiral is perpendicular to the anvil and hammer
    the straight end of the wire to flatten it. Remove the
    spiral shape from the anvil. With round-nose pliers,
    create a small, open spiral on the flat end of the wire.

4   Repeat step 2 using the 4½" (11.5cm) and 5½" (14cm)
    pieces of wire. Hammer the 4½" (11.5cm) piece as in
    step 3. Hammer the spiral on the 5½" (14cm) piece,
    but *do not* flip this wire; simply hammer the middle of
    the 5½" (14cm) wire piece lightly and then flatten the
    end of the wire fully.

5   With round-nose pliers, grasp the flattened end of the 5½" (14cm) spiral shape and create a simple loop toward the back of the spiral shape.

6   Place all 3 spiral shapes inside the teardrop loop-and-lock frame, with the looped shape in the middle. Be sure that they all fit in neatly and that the spirals touch the inside of the frame.

7   Keeping the spirals against the frame edge, pinch them together with your nondominant hand. Use one 3" (7.5cm) piece of 22-gauge wire to tightly bind all 3 spiral shapes together, wrapping them 7 times.

8   With chain-nose pliers, gently open the frame loops and the center spiral shape loop by twisting them to the side. Insert 1 link of chain (or attach a jump ring) onto the 3 open loops. Close the loops.

9   Measure approximately 1" (2.5cm) from the top of the frame and tightly wrap a 30" (76cm) piece of 26-gauge wire 10 times around the frame, ending the last wrap at the back of the frame.

10 Slide 1 bead onto the wire and wrap the wire down and around the frame 10 times. Continue wrapping beads to the frame in this way, weaving the wire through the spirals where necessary to attach the spirals to the frame. After you have wrapped about 11 beads to the frame, wrap the wire around the frame 10 times to secure, ending directly opposite your first wrap.

    With chain-nose pliers, pinch the excess wire tightly to the frame. With wire cutters, trim the excess wire.

11 Attach an ear wire to the link of chain.

12 Repeat steps 1–11 to make the second earring.

a perfect spiral

To ensure a perfect spiral, begin by making sure the tail-end of the wire is flat. This flat end ensures that your swirl will begin with a perfectly round loop, which will continue to be perfectly round as it spirals. You can attain this flat end in several ways.

Perhaps the simplest way is to use ultra-flush cutters. Ultra-flush cutters have very little "pinch" because the edges and angles of the jaws have less of an incline than most wire cutters.

You can use regular wire cutters if you pay attention to the angle of the jaws. When you cut a piece of wire with the jaws facing in one direction, the wire will angle toward that direction. To "neutralize" this effect: Make one cut, then switch the direction of the cutter and make a second cut. The second cut creates a flat edge.

Ellen earrings, back view.

Note: If you would like your earrings to be mirror images, as shown, rather than matching, switch the directions of the spirals before you attach them to the second earring frame.

PENELOPE

The Penelope earring is the only project in this
book in which the ear wire is an integral part
of the frame. No need for separate ear wires.
Although I chose a teardrop frame for this design,
the technique also works great for hoops.

The real reason I am in love with this earring,
however, is the way the design creates a "wall" of
color across the frame. I have used variations of
sapphire to create an ombré effect, as the sapphire
stone naturally comes in a variety of shades, from
light blue to dark blue to sparkling cobalt. It is
not uncommon to find strands of sapphire for sale
already in this beautiful color formation.

time
30–45 minutes per pair

technique
simple loop (page 32)

tools
round-nose pliers
chain-nose pliers
wire cutters
permanent marker
¾" (2cm) mandrel
standard hammer
anvil
ruler

materials
12" (30.5cm) of 20-gauge gold-filled wire
60" (152.5cm) of 26-gauge gold-filled wire
three hundred twenty 1mm microfaceted
  sapphire rondelles of varying shades

finished size
2¾" x 1¾" (7cm x 4.5cm)

Note: Beads may vary slightly in size, so the number of beads per row will never be definite, whether you're threading beads onto wire for this project or wrapping stacks of beads for designs later in the book.

TO PREP *(for 1 earring)*

Cut one 6" (15cm) piece of 20-gauge wire and mark it 2" (5cm) from one end of the wire with a permanent marker.
Cut one 30" (76cm) piece of 26-gauge wire.
Select 160 beads and organize from light to dark to create an ombré effect.

TO MAKE

1   With chain-nose pliers, grasp the 6" (15cm) piece of wire at the mark and bend the wire to a 45-degree angle. With round-nose pliers, grasp the short tail-end of the wire and bend it perpendicular to create a hook.

2   Place the long tail-end against the mandrel so that the 45-degree angle is at the top. Wrap the wire around the mandrel, creating a teardrop shape. Create a simple loop at the curved end of the wire and push the hook through the loop. Place the frame on the anvil and lightly hammer, avoiding the loop and hook.

3   With chain-nose pliers, hold the 30" (76cm) piece of 26-gauge wire about ¼" (6mm) from the loop along the curved part of the frame. Wrap the wire 5 times around the frame.

4   Slide enough beads onto the 26-gauge wire to cover the width of the frame (approximately 30 beads), working from light to dark in your color palette. Wrap the tail 5 times around the other side of the frame to secure the first row of beads. Continue sliding on beads and wrapping 5 times around the frame in alternate directions between each row of beads until you reach the bottom of the frame. Try to mimic the color change from each previous row to achieve a consistent "wall" of color, from light to dark across all rows. (You should end up with approximately 8 rows of beads.)

5   Repeat steps 1–4 to make the second earring.

GISELE

Named after the gorgeous long-and-lean model Gisele Bündchen, this earring has received its fair share of fame, as it is also a favorite of Britney Spears and has been featured in many bridal magazines. The Gisele earring combines several techniques, including attaching frames, attaching bead dangles to chain, and layering beads to create bead cluster drops. These layers make it a fun project to play with, colorwise.

Naturally, you can choose beads in a monochromatic color scheme, but you may also want to create an ombré effect (page 59). Or you might just want to choose a combination of bead colors that speaks to you. Just as supermodels look great in whatever they wear, this earring design can support any color combination you dream up.

time
45–60 minutes per pair

techniques
looped-ends horseshoe frame (page 29)
single wrapped loop (page 33)
double wrapped loop (page 34)
teardrop loop and wrap (page 35)
eye pin (page 38)
bead cluster drops (page 75)

tools
round-nose pliers
2 pairs of chain-nose pliers
wire cutters
¼" (6mm) mandrel
½" (13mm) mandrel
ruler

materials
12" (30.5cm) of 16-gauge gold-filled wire
80" (203cm) of 24-gauge gold-filled wire
55 links of gold-filled dainty chain
thirty-eight 3mm faceted watermelon
  tourmaline rondelles of assorted colors
two 4mm faceted gold round beads
two 4mm x 8mm green apatite briolettes
1 pair of gold-filled ear wires

finished size
3" x 1" (10cm x 2.5cm)

TO PREP *(for 1 earring)*

Cut one 2½" (6.5cm) piece of 16-gauge wire,
  one 3½" (9cm) piece of 16-gauge wire, and
  twenty 2" (5cm) pieces of 24-gauge wire.
Cut two 5-link pieces and one 15-link piece
  of chain.

TO MAKE

1   Create a looped-ends horseshoe frame using the
    ¼" (6mm) mandrel and the 2½" (6.5cm) piece of
    16-gauge wire. (This frame will become the top
    portion of the earring.)

2   Create a looped-ends horseshoe frame using the
    ½" (13mm) mandrel and the 3½" (9cm) piece
    of 16-gauge wire, curving the wire into a subtle
    teardrop shape. (This frame will become the bottom
    portion of the earring.)

3   Create an eye pin from a 2" (5cm) piece of 24-gauge
    wire. Slide on a rondelle and use a single wrapped
    loop to close, making sure that the circumference of
    the loop is large enough to slide onto 16-gauge wire.
    With wire cutters, trim the excess wire.

    Repeat this step to create 15 wrapped-loop dangles
    in total. (This step creates all the individual dangles
    needed for 1 earring.)

4   Begin a double wrapped loop with another 2" (5cm)
    piece of 24-gauge wire, but *before closing the loop*,
    insert 3 bead dangles from step 3. Wrap to close,
    then slide a rondelle onto the wire tail. Create the
    final wrapped loop to close.

    Repeat twice. (This step creates all the bead cluster
    drops needed for 1 earring.)

5   Create a kind of eye pin using techniques from the teardrop loop and wrap: Slide a briolette onto a 2" (5cm) piece of 24-gauge wire and fold both ends of the wire upward over the bead to cross each other. With chain-nose pliers in your nondominant hand, hold the crossed wires in place. Slide a gold faceted bead onto the wire. Begin a loop above the bead, but *before closing the loop*, insert the center link of the 15-link chain onto the loop (at the 8th link). Wrap to close. With wire cutters, trim the excess wire.

6   With chain-nose pliers, gently open the loops on the looped-ends frame. Insert 2 bead dangles, 1 cluster drop, 1 bead dangle, 1 bead cluster drop, 1 bead dangle, 1 bead cluster drop, and 2 bead dangles. (These dangles and drops should hang from the bottom of the frame.) *Before closing the loop,* hook this frame onto the small frame.

7   With chain-nose pliers, gently open the loops on the top frame. Insert the end links of the 15-link chain into each loop, making sure the chain isn't twisted and that the teardrop briolette hangs freely over the front of the frames. *Do not* close the loops.

8   Insert 1 end of the 5-link chain onto 1 loop of the small frame, and then insert 1 end of another 5-link chain onto the other loop. With chain-nose pliers, close the loops.

9   Begin a double wrapped loop with a 2" (5cm) piece of 24-gauge wire, but *before closing the loop*, insert the end links of the 2 pieces of 5-link chain onto the loop. Wrap to close, making sure that the chains are not twisted, then slide a rondelle onto the wire tail. Create the final wrapped loop to close. This dangle will act as a bead link, connecting the ear wire to the earring.

10   Attach an ear wire to the bead-link dangle and, with wire cutters, trim the excess wire.

11   Repeat steps 1–10 to make the second earring.

combining gemstone beads

When you choose more than one type of gemstone bead to include in a design, you must think about more than just color scheme. You must also consider their relative hardness. Most people know that a diamond (among other things) can cut through glass. That's one tough gemstone! But not all gems have this ability, and some gemstones are easier to scratch or damage than others. The last thing you want to do is stack one bead on top of another, only to discover that one quickly becomes damaged. To compare the relative hardness of any gemstones, use Mohs' scale, which ranks stones from soft to hard using values of 1 to 10. Any gemstone will scratch another that is lower on Mohs' scale. A stone's hardness will also affect its care. For more information on cleaning and protecting your gemstone jewelry, see page 158.

CALYPSO

The Calypso earrings are a lot of earring with little effort—made with just one piece of wire! You'll loop, bend, and twist it to create a double spiral within a half-teardrop shape. I made the sample Calypso earrings in sterling silver to show you how to use a compound called liver of sulfur to add depth and distinction to the metal's patina.

time
10–15 minutes per pair

technique
simple loop (page 32)

tools
round-nose pliers
chain-nose pliers
wire cutters
standard and chasing hammers
    (or ball-peen hammer)
anvil
permanent marker
ruler

materials
24" (61cm) of 16-gauge sterling silver
    wire
5 links of sterling silver common chain
1 pair of sterling silver ear wires
liver of sulfur materials (optional)

finished size
2½" x 1¾" (6.5cm x 4.5cm)

TO PREP *(for 1 earring)*

Cut one 12" (30.5cm) piece of 16-gauge wire.
Cut one 2-link piece of chain.

TO MAKE

1 With round-nose pliers, create a simple loop on 1 end of the 12" (30.5cm) piece of 16-gauge wire. With chain-nose pliers, grasp the small loop flat between its jaws. Using your fingers for leverage, rotate the chain-nose pliers approximately 4 times away from you to create a spiral shape. (a)

2 Mark the wire approximately 1" (2.5cm) from the bottom of the spiral with a permanent marker. With round-nose pliers, grasp the wire at this mark and wrap the wire around and down your tool to create a loop. (The wire should extend beyond the spiral.) Insert a 2-link piece of chain onto the loop. (b)

3 Repeat step 1 at the end of the wire, spiraling 7 times in the reverse direction so that the spirals curve toward each other. (c)

4 With your fingers, bend the larger spiral in and under the smaller one, creating a teardrop shape.

5 Place the earring on the anvil and hammer to flare and texture the earring.

6 If desired, oxidize the earring to achieve an antiqued effect, as shown in the photo. See How to Work with Liver of Sulfur for complete instructions (opposite).

7 Attach an ear wire to the top link of chain.

8 Repeat steps 1–7 to make the second earring.

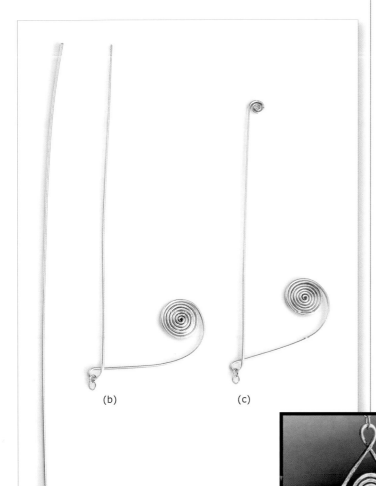

(b)

(c)

(a)

how to work with liver of sulfur

Liver of sulfur is a mixture of potassium sulfides that chemically react with the surface of some metals, producing a gray to black effect. To create this patina, you will need a jar or ceramic bowl, access to water, rubber gloves, tongs, and stainless steel wool (to clean the earrings after their sulfur bath). Look for liver of sulfur at jewelry stores or online.

To make the sulfur bath, place a fingernail-size portion of liver of sulfur in a jar and add 1½ cups (360ml) warm water. Stir the mixture with tongs until the liver of sulfur has completely dissolved. Then drop your earrings into the jar. When they have turned black, remove them with tongs and run them under cold water to remove all liver of sulfur from the earrings. Allow the earrings to air-dry. Wearing rubber gloves, gently buff them clean with stainless steel wool. (I suggest wearing rubber gloves when working with the steel wool, because steel wool can irritate your hands.) Voilà, you now have a rich, weathered patina on your brand-new earrings!

Note: Pearls and coral have sensitive, porous outer coverings that are easily damaged by liver of sulfur. If you have a design with these beads that you want to antique, I suggest carefully brushing the liver of sulfur onto the metal with a small paintbrush, avoiding the beads. Rinse thoroughly with cold water when finished, then clean with stainless steel wool.

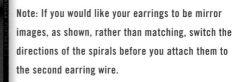

Note: If you would like your earrings to be mirror images, as shown, rather than matching, switch the directions of the spirals before you attach them to the second earring wire.

KELLY

I cannot claim to be the creator to this design, as its origins are thought to be Greco-Roman. The double-spiral design represents the equinoxes, when day and night are of equal length, so it seems natural that they would also represent balance—a trait you'll need to successfully complete this earring design.

Once you have the technique down, it might be fun to experiment with using different gauges of wire, or connecting them through the center "figure eights" with jump rings to make links for a chain, or even wrapping a stone in the center.

time
15–20 minutes per pair

techniques
simple loop (page 32)
teardrop loop and wrap (page 35)
jump rings (page 39)

tools
round-nose pliers
2 pairs of chain-nose pliers
wire cutters
standard hammer
anvil
ruler

materials
57" (145cm) of 18-gauge gold-filled wire
6" (15cm) of 24-gauge gold-filled wire
two 5mm x 6mm lapis lazuli briolettes
1 pair of gold-filled ear wires
eight 7mm jump rings (optional)

finished size
3" x 1½" (7.5cm x 3.8cm)

TO PREP *(for 1 earring)*

Cut one 10" (25.5cm) piece of
    18-gauge wire and mark at 5½" (14cm)
    with a permanent marker.
Cut one 8½" (21.5cm) piece of
    18-gauge wire and mark at 4¾" (12cm)
    with a permanent marker.
Cut one 6" (15cm) piece of 18-gauge wire and
    mark at 3½" (9cm) with a permanent marker.
Cut one 3" (7.5cm) piece of 24-gauge wire and one 4" piece
    of 18-gauge wire, if making jump rings.

TO MAKE

1   With round-nose pliers, grasp the 10" (25.5cm) piece
    of wire at the 5½" (14cm) mark. Wrap the longer end
    of your wire around the middle of one jaw of the pliers,
    creating a simple loop.

2   Flip over the piece of wire and create another loop,
    wrapping the longer end right underneath the first loop.
    (You should now have a figure 8 in the center of your
    wire, and both ends should be equal in length.) (This
    step creates the large frame.)

3   Repeat steps 1–2 with the 8½" (21.5cm) and the 6"
    (15cm) pieces of 18-gauge wire, grasping each at its
    mark and wrapping to create figure-8 loops. (This step
    creates the medium and small frames.)

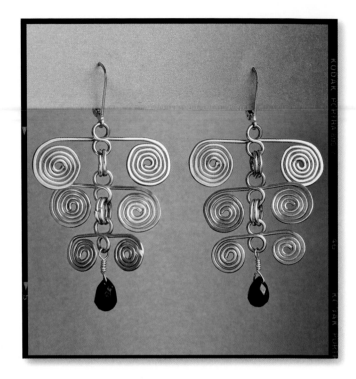

4 With round-nose pliers, loop the end of the largest frame under, toward the center of the frame. With chain-nose pliers, grasp the small loop flat between the jaws of the pliers. Rotate the chain-nose pliers approximately 5 times away from you to create a spiral shape.

Repeat on the other end of the wire, making sure that the spiral shapes are even on both sides.

5 Repeat step 4 with the medium and small frames, spiraling 4 turns on the medium frame ends and 3 turns on the small frame ends.

6 Place each frame on an anvil and hammer lightly to flare, being careful to only lightly tap the figure-8 loops.

7 Create a jump ring by wrapping 4" (10cm) of 18-gauge wire around the middle of the round-nose pliers and cutting the wire with wire cutters where it meets in a perfect circle. Repeat 3 times to create 4 jump rings in total. (Or, use premade jump rings.)

8 With 2 pairs of chain-nose pliers, open the jump rings by holding both sides of each jump ring and twisting it open. Attach 2 jump rings to the bottom loop on the large frame and to the top loop on the medium frame. Close the rings. Use 2 more jump rings to attach the bottom loop of the medium frame to the top loop of the small frame. Close the rings.

9 With a 3" (7.5cm) piece of 24-gauge wire, form a teardrop loop and wrap around a briolette. Begin the loop above the bead, but *before closing the loop*, insert the bottom loop of the smallest frame onto the briolette loop. Wrap to close. With wire cutters, trim the excess wire.

10 Attach an ear wire to the top loop of the largest frame.

11 Repeat steps 1–10 to make the second earring.

EDIE

Abracadabra—I will wave this magic wand and change this piece of silk into a gorgeous lightweight earring! One, two, three . . . poof!

Okay, you won't really need a special wand to create the Edie earrings, but this design may just feel a little like magic. All you need is a bit of thin, malleable fabric, some wire, chain, fabric tape, patience and . . . you can transform/recycle/convert/ evolve a simple piece of fabric into an earring. You know that skirt that you love that fits a bit too tightly around the waist? What about that T-shirt you wore to your first rock concert? Make them into earrings! This earring project is a great way to change any piece of clothing in your closet into an accessory.

time

50–60 minutes per pair

techniques

simple loop (page 32)

tools

round-nose pliers
2 pairs of chain-nose pliers
wire cutters
½" (13mm) mandrel
1" (2.5cm) mandrel
standard hammer
anvil
permanent marker
ruler
scissors

materials

24" (61cm) of 18-gauge wire
32" (81cm) of 24-gauge gold-filled wire
26" (66cm) of gold-filled simple chain
3 links of gold-filled common chain or two
  4.5mm jump rings
36" (91cm) of ¾"-wide (2cm-wide) double-
  stick fabric tape
two 18" x 1" (45.5cm x 2.5cm) pieces of
  sari fabric (or any fabric)
1 pair of ear wires

finished size

2 ¾" x 2" (7cm x 3.8cm)

Note: Use inexpensive craft wire to make this frame—your fabric will be covering it. Just make sure that the wire gauge is at least as heavy as in the materials list (otherwise, the earring will be fragile).

TO PREP *(for 1 earring)*

Cut one 12" (30.5cm) piece of 18-gauge
  wire and mark it at 7" (18cm) with a
  permanent marker.
Cut two 8" (20.5cm) pieces of
  24-gauge wire.
Cut one 13" (33cm) piece of simple chain
  and one 1-link piece of common chain, if using.
Cut one 18" (45.5cm) piece of ¾" (2cm) fabric tape.

TO MAKE

1   Create a simple loop at the shorter, 5" (12.5cm) end of the 12" (30.5cm) piece of 18-gauge wire. Place the ½" (13mm) mandrel between the loop and the 7" (18cm) mark, and wrap both ends around the mandrel until the loop and the mark meet in the center. (This will create a teardrop shape.) (a)

2   With chain-nose pliers, grasp the wire at the 7" (18cm) mark and bend the wire down to a 45-degree angle.

3   Place the 1" (2.5cm) mandrel at the center of the 7" (18cm) tail and, with your fingers, wrap the wire around the mandrel until it meets at the 45-degree angle. (b)

4   With chain-nose pliers, create an open loop on the end of the wire and gently bend it down until it is horizontal to the earring frame. Use the open loop to hook and attach onto both parts of the frame. Close the loop to secure the frame into place. (c)

5   Place the frame on an anvil and lightly hammer evenly throughout to flare, being careful to avoid the loops.

6   Lay one 18" x 1" (45.5cm x 2.5cm) piece of fabric flat on the table, wrong side facing up, and carefully apply the 18" (45.5cm) piece of ¾" (2cm) fabric tape down the

center of the strip, making sure the tape is smooth and does not have wrinkles. Fold over the ends of the fabric onto the edges of the tape on all sides, so that the sticky tape is exposed in the middle of the fabric only.

7   Just below the top loops on 1 end of the frame, begin gently wrapping the fabric around the frame so that the tape adheres to the frame. Wrap the fabric all the way around the frame, overlapping slightly as necessary. With scissors, cut off any excess fabric. (d)

8   At the top loop, begin wrapping an 8" (20.5cm) piece of 24-gauge wire down the frame to tightly secure the fabric to the frame. Leave a 1" (2.5cm) wire tail to attach to the chain.

Repeat on the other side of the frame with the other 8" (20.5cm) piece of 24-gauge wire.

9   Attach the end link of a 13" (33cm) piece of chain to 1 of the wire tails, then finish wrapping the tail to the frame. With chain-nose pliers, pinch the wire tightly to the frame.

10   Wrap the chain around the frame, evenly spacing the wraps 3 times around 1 side, 3 times around the bottom, and 3 times around the other side. Attach the end link of the chain to the remaining 1" (2.5cm) wire tail and finish wrapping the tail to the frame. With chain-nose pliers, pinch the wire tightly to the frame. (e)

11   With chain-nose pliers, gently open the top loop of the frame by twisting it to the side. Insert 1 link of common chain (or attach a jump ring) onto the loop. Close the loop. Attach an ear wire to the link of chain. With wire cutters, trim the excess wire.

12   Repeat steps 1–11 to make the second earring.

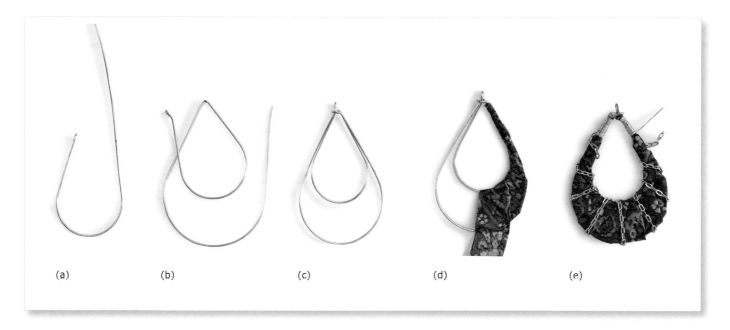

(a)   (b)   (c)   (d)   (e)

Chapter 5

When a Glamour Girl walks into the room, heads turn. Confident, strong, and alluring, she brings the "wow" to the party—and her accessories are no exception. From the smoldering look of Hollywood icon Elizabeth Taylor to the sexy modern looks of women such as Kate Moss, Nicole Kidman, and Victoria Beckham, glamour has many faces. That's why, in the pages that follow, you'll find a glamorous mix of old Hollywood style and looks for a hot night out.

GLAMOUR GIRL

In this chapter you will continue to explore designs with unusual frame shapes, discovering how it feels to gently coerce wire without the use of a mandrel. You will also learn about asymmetry and how it can be used to create optical illusions of length. Finally, you will go deep into the technique of wrapping stacks of beads, which can be used in fun and exciting ways to amp up the glamour quotient.

"In the pages that follow, you'll find a glamorous mix of old Hollywood style and looks for a hot night out."

Taipei® polypropylene blend by Highland Court; highlandcourtfabrics.com.

Amethyst gold-leaf drawer pulls by Eduardo Garza; eduardogarza.com.

Coin, Diamond Bandelle

The rich and regal jewel tone takes center stage this...

HARLOW

"Lights, camera, glamour!" The wisps of chain, the gorgeous pearl—so old Hollywood. Named after Hollywood's original blond sex symbol, Jean Harlow, these earrings move with a grace and a flair that will be sure to get you noticed. If I were living in the 1940s, I would accessorize with earrings just like Harlow—long, draped, sexy, and fun. So unleash your old Hollywood glamour girl with this design—and don't be surprised if people start mistaking you for a celebrity!

time

5–10 minutes per pair

techniques

double wrapped loop (page 34)

tools

round-nose pliers
2 pairs of chain-nose pliers
wire cutters
ruler

materials

4" (10cm) of 24-gauge gold-filled wire
two 8mm coin pearl beads
84 links of dainty chain
1 pair of ear wires

finished size

2½" x ½" (7.5cm x 13mm)

TO PREP *(for 1 earring)*

Cut one 2" (5cm) piece of 24-gauge wire.
Cut one 11-link piece, one 13-link piece, and one 15-link
   piece of chain.

TO MAKE

1 Begin a double wrapped loop with a 2" (5 cm) piece
   of wire, but *before closing the loop*, insert the end links
   of the 3 pieces of chain in any order onto the loop.
   Wrap to close. With wire cutters, trim the excess wire.
   Slide a bead onto the tail-end of the wire and create the
   final wrapped loop to close. With wire cutters, trim the
   excess wire.

2 With chain-nose pliers, attach an ear wire to the top
   loop.

3 Repeat steps 1–2 to make the second earring.

gifts from the sea

*Until the 1970s, only natural pearls were used in jewelry making, and jewelry
with this material was highly prized and expensive. But amazing advances have
taken place in the pearl industry, and cultured pearls are now common. This
breakthrough has produced a variety of shapes never seen in nature, including
long, sticklike pearls and diamond shaped pearls, and I have even seen a pearl
in the shape of a Buddha! Whether you choose natural or cultured pearls, have
fun designing with the many shapes, sizes, and styles of pearl beads available.*

GWYNETH

Nothing says "glamour" quite like a pair of
stilettos—and that's just one reason why the
Gwyneth earrings' attention-getting stiletto style
is perfect for an evening out. This particular
design is manipulated by hand, organic in nature,
and will likely look a bit different each time you
make it. But there is no "wrong" way to make it!
So grab your stilettos, put on your tool belt, and
create away!

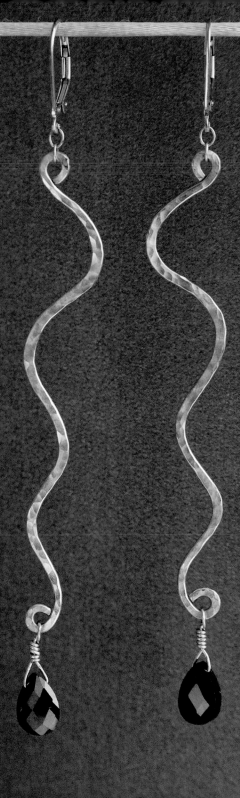

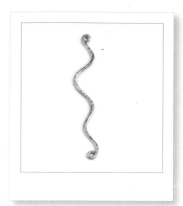

time

5–10 minutes per pair

techniques

simple loop (page 32)
teardrop loop and wrap (page 35)

tools

round-nose pliers
2 pairs of chain-nose pliers
wire cutters
standard and chasing hammers
   (or ball-peen hammer)
anvil
ruler

materials

7" (18 cm) of 16-gauge gold-filled wire
4" (10cm) of 24-gauge gold-filled wire
5 links of dainty chain
two 4mm x 6mm jet cubic zirconia
   briolettes
1 pair of ear wires

finished size

3¼" x ¼" (8cm x 6mm)

TO PREP *(for 1 earring)*

Cut one 3½" (9cm) piece of 16-gauge wire
   and one 2" (5cm) piece of 24-gauge wire.
Cut one 2-link piece of chain.

TO MAKE

1   With round-nose pliers, create a simple loop on each end of the 3½" (9cm) piece of 16-gauge wire, making sure the 2 loops face in opposite directions.

2   With your fingers or round-nose pliers, create 3 gentle waves in the wire in a free-form pattern.

3   Place the frame on the anvil and lightly hammer it, first with the standard side of the hammer to flatten and then with the chasing side to lightly tap texture onto 1 side of the wire.

4   Slide a briolette onto the 2" (5cm) piece of 24-gauge wire and form a teardrop loop and wrap.

5   With chain-nose pliers, gently open the loops on both ends of the frame by twisting the wire toward yourself. At one end of the frame, insert the teardrop dangle created in step 4. At the other end of the frame, insert a chain link.

6   Close both loops. Attach an ear wire to the top link of the chain.

7   Repeat steps 1–6 to make the second earring.

SALMA

Hello, curves! This stiletto earring busts out in
all directions! Named after the beautiful queen of
curves, Salma Hayak, the Salma earrings evoke
voluptuous, sexy energy. All the curves are created
by hand—no two earrings will ever be exactly the
same—so you have freedom to experiment and
explore.

time

15–20 minutes per pair

techniques

simple loop (page 32)
crossover loop-and-lock teardrop frame
   (page 31)
single wrapped loop (page 33)
teardrop loop and wrap (page 35)
eye pin (page 38)

tools

round-nose pliers
2 pairs of chain-nose pliers
wire cutters
standard hammer
anvil
¼" (6mm) mandrel
ballpoint pen
ruler

materials

14" (35.5cm) of 16-gauge gold-filled wire
12" (30.5cm) of 24-gauge gold-filled wire
four 6mm garnet rounds
two 4mm x 6mm garnet briolettes
3 links common chain or two 4.5mm jump
   rings
1 pair of ear wires

finished size

3¾" x ¾" (9.5cm x 2cm)

TO PREP *(for 1 earring)*

Cut one 7" (18cm) piece of 16-gauge wire
   and mark it at 1¼", 2¼", 3¾", 5¼", and
   6¼" (3cm, 5.5cm, 9.5cm, 14.5cm, and
   15.5cm) with the marker.
Cut three 2" (5cm) pieces of 24-gauge wire.
Cut one 1-link piece of chain, if using.

TO MAKE

1   Place the ¼" (6mm) mandrel at the 3¾"
    (9.5cm) mark of the 16-gauge wire. With
    your fingers, wrap both ends of the wire
    around the mandrel to cross at the 2¼"
    (5.5cm) and 5¼" (14.5cm) marks.

2   Place the ballpoint pen at the crossover point
    and use it as a mandrel. With your fingers,
    wrap both ends of the wire up and over to cross at 1¼"
    (3cm) and 6¼" (15.5cm) marks. Create simple loops
    and finish the frame following steps 2–6 of the crossover
    loop-and-lock teardrop frame.

3   Place the frame on the anvil and gently tap the crossover
    points with the hammer.

4   With a 2" (5cm) piece of 24-gauge wire, form a teardrop
    loop and wrap around a briolette. Begin the loop above
    the bead, but *before closing the loop*, attach this bead
    dangle to the bottom of the frame. Wrap to close. With
    wire cutters, trim the excess wire.

5   Create an eye pin from another 2" (5cm) piece of
    24-gauge wire. Slide a 6mm bead onto the eye pin.
    Begin a single wrapped loop large enough to fit around
    the crossover point of the frame, but *before closing the
    loop*, insert the open loop around the lowest crossover
    point of the frame. Wrap to close. With wire cutters, trim
    the excess wire.

6   Repeat step 5 to create a second bead dangle, but insert
    the open loop around the top crossover point of the
    frame instead of the lowest crossover point.

7   With chain-nose pliers, gently open the top loop of the
    frame and insert 1 link of chain (or attach a jump ring).
    Close the loop and attach an ear wire to the link of chain.

8   Repeat steps 1–7 to make the second earring.

ANNE

As I write this book, I am sitting in a café wearing a black one-shouldered dress. I love asymmetry and am always attracted to things that are "a bit off." However, there's more to an asymmetrical design than just novelty; it also tricks the eye, creating the illusion of length against the body. Asymmetrical earrings, like Anne, incline along the slope of the neck, making yours seem long, slender, and oh, so glamorous.

As you make these and other earrings, play around with the concept of asymmetry. To achieve the greatest lengthening effect, always wear the long side toward the neck.

time
20–30 minutes (per pair)

techniques
simple loop (page 32)
double wrapped loop (page 34)
teardrop loop and wrap (page 35)
wrapping single beads (page 36)

tools
round-nose pliers
2 pairs of chain-nose pliers
wire cutters
standard hammer
anvil
ruler

materials
7" (18cm) of 16-gauge gold-filled wire
8" (20.5cm) of 24-gauge gold-filled wire
30" (76cm) of 26-gauge gold-filled wire
60 links of common chain
four 4mm x 6mm champagne cubic zirconia
*   briolettes*
twelve 3mm champagne pearl rounds
1 pair of ear wires

finished size
3¾" x 1½" (9.5cm x 3.8cm)

TO PREP *(for 1 earring)*

Cut one 3½" (9cm) piece of 16-gauge
    wire, two 2" (5cm) pieces of 24-gauge
    wire, one 13" (33cm) piece of 26-gauge
    wire, and one 2" (5cm) piece of
    26-gauge wire.
Cut one 12-link and one 18-link
    piece of chain.

**Note: If you would like your earrings to be mirror
images, as shown, rather than matching, reverse
the order in which you add the linked chain in steps
5–6 when making the second earring**

TO MAKE

1   With round-nose pliers, create simple loops
    on both ends of the 3½" (9cm) wire; one loop
    should curve upward and the other downward.
    Shape the frame by holding your thumb
    against 1 loop and gently pushing that loop up
    over your thumbnail. Repeat with the opposite
    loop to make a slightly curved bar frame.

2   Place the frame on the anvil and hammer flat.

3   Place 1 end of the 13" (33cm) piece of wire
    next to a loop. Wrap the length of the wire around the
    frame so that the long wire tail extends toward the front
    of the frame. Slide a 3mm bead onto the wire and secure
    it to the front of the frame with 5 wraps. Continue adding
    beads using the technique of wrapping single beads until
    you near the opposite loop (about 5 beads), wrapping 5
    times between each bead and ending with a wire wrap.
    With chain-nose pliers, pinch the excess wire tightly to
    the frame. With wire cutters, trim the excess wire.

4   With a 2" (5cm) piece of 24-gauge wire, form a teardrop
    loop and wrap on a briolette. Repeat to create another
    briolette dangle.

5   With chain-nose pliers, open the simple loop on 1 end of
    frame. Insert the briolette dangle and 1 end link of the
    18-link chain. Close the simple loop.

6   With chain-nose pliers, open the simple loop on the other
    end of the frame. Insert the end link of the 12-link chain
    and the other briolette dangle. Close the simple loop.

7   Begin a double wrapped loop with the 2" (5cm) piece
    of wire, but *before closing the loop*, insert the 2 ends of
    chain. Wrap to close, being careful not to twist the chain.
    Slide on a 3mm bead and create the final wrapped loop
    to close. With wire cutters, trim the excess wire. With
    chain-nose pliers, attach an ear wire to the top loop.

8   Repeat steps 1–7 to make the second earring.

RIO

The fabulous Rio earring is as fun and sexy as the city it is named after! Inspired by shattered glass, this design uses the wrapping stacks of beads technique. In the years since its debut with Double Happiness Jewelry, this earring design has taken on a life of its own, inspiring countless others to create earrings mimicking its style.

The technique is quite tactile, so give yourself time to get it right. With practice you will become adept at stacking beads perfectly straight. Then, have fun! The technique's applications are many, and you will see other ways to use it in the earrings that follow in this chapter.

time
45–50 minutes per pair

techniques
crossover loop-and-lock hoop frame
    (page 30)
wrapping stacks of beads (page 37)

tools
round-nose pliers
2 pairs of chain-nose pliers
wire cutters
1¼" (3cm) mandrel
standard hammer
anvil
ruler

materials
14" (35.5cm) of 16-gauge gold-filled
    wire
60" (152.5cm) of 26-gauge gold-filled
    wire
140 3mm silver metal faceted beads
3 links of common chain or two 4.5mm
    jump rings
1 pair of ear wires

finished size
3" x 2" (7.5cm x 5cm)

TO PREP *(for 1 earring)*

Cut one 7" (18cm) piece of 16-gauge wire and one 30" (76cm) piece of 26-gauge wire.
Cut 1 link of chain, if using.

TO MAKE

1   Create a crossover loop-and-lock hoop frame using the 1¼" (3cm) mandrel and the 7" (18cm) piece of 16-gauge wire.

2   Place the 30" (76cm) piece of 26-gauge wire at the center of the left side of the frame. Wrap the wire around the frame 4 times, making sure to wrap the wire while holding the frame right side up, so the wire will be hidden behind the beads as you wrap. Slide 1 bead onto the wire and grip it against the frame with your fingers. Pull the wire down behind the bead, tightly wrapping twice around the frame. (a)

3   Continue adding beads using the technique of wrapping stacks of beads to a frame. Add beads In the following pattern: 1-1-2-1-2-3-4-5-6-7 (center bead stack)-6-5-4-3-2-1-2-1-1-1. End with 4 wraps, making sure that it is evenly lined up with the other side. With chain-nose pliers, pinch the wire tightly to the frame. With wire cutters, trim the excess wire. (b, c)

4   With chain-nose pliers, gently open the top loop of the frame and insert 1 link of common chain (or attach a jump ring). Close loop. Attach an ear wire to the chain link.

5   Repeat steps 1–4 to make the second earring.

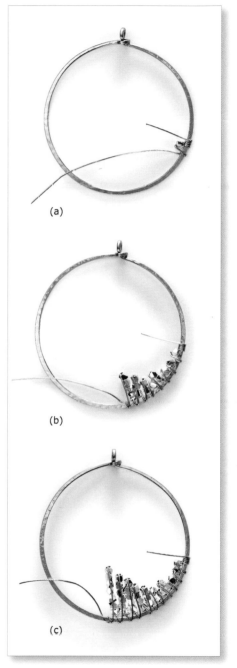

(a)

(b)

(c)

all that glitters

When wrapping stacks of beads, you'll find that you can create a new look just by changing the beads you use. The Rio earrings go from a glittering metal show-stopper to a sleek, cool, downtown accessory when lapis beads take center stage, as shown here.

I also had fun playing around with heavy metals, changing the look of the Nicole and Solace earrings (pages 118 and 124). You can use different colors, perhaps creating an ombré effect, or mix up the colors all together. Which look do you like best?

A mixture of bead types and cuts would also show an amazing display of beauty and contrast. I think the challenge when mixing bead types and cuts is to maintain some relationship between all the beads to bring the look harmoniously together. So play around with your materials to find color and bead combinations that best suit your style.

DREW

When I was a teenager, my grandparents went
to Peru and came back with an amazing pair of
earrings just for me. Although they were heavy
and much too sophisticated for a fifteen-year-old,
I wore those earrings every day of my sophomore
year. Their design was simple: A large chrysocolla
bead gleamed at the top, and a metal engraving of
a pre-Columbian sun god descended downward
in a bladelike shape. These earrings cemented my
obsession with the power and beauty of jewelry,
and so I have designed a modern-day version.
These Drew earrings evoke antiquity with a
thoroughly modern twist. Their long, graceful
necks taper into a semicircular shape that is both
unique and flattering. This unusual design is sure
to get you noticed—whether you are a fresh fifteen
or a fabulous fifty.

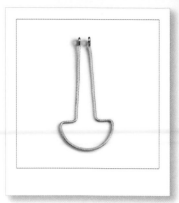

time

50–60 minutes per pair

technique

simple loop (page 32)

tools

round-nose pliers
2 pairs of chain-nose pliers
wire cutters
½" (13mm) mandrel
standard hammer
anvil
permanent marker
ruler

materials

14" (35.5cm) of 16-gauge
 gold-filled wire
8" (20.5cm) of 24-gauge
 gold-filled wire
60" (152.5cm) of 26-gauge
 gold-filled wire
sixty-four 2mm round brass beads
two 4mm x 8mm garnet nuggets
3 links of solid chain or two 6mm
 jump rings
1 pair of ear wires

finished size

2¾" x 1½" (7cm x 3.8cm)

TO PREP *(for 1 earring)*

Cut one 7" (18cm) piece of 16-gauge wire and
  mark it at 2¼", 2½", 4½", and 4¾"
  (5.5cm, 6.5cm, 11.5cm, and 12cm) with the
  permanent marker.
Cut one 4" (10cm) piece of 24-gauge wire and one 30"
  (76cm) piece of 26-gauge wire.
Cut 1 link of chain, if using.

TO MAKE

1   Place the ½" (13mm) mandrel on the 7" (18cm) piece
    of 16-gauge wire between the 2½" (6.5cm) and the 4½"
    (11.5cm) marks. With your fingers, wrap the wire around
    the mandrel, creating a U shape.

2   With chain-nose pliers, grasp the wire at the 2¼"
    (5.5cm) mark and bend the wire toward the center of the
    frame, creating a 90-degree angle. Repeat at the 4½"
    (11.5cm) mark.

3   With chain-nose pliers, grasp the wire at the 2½"
    (5.5cm) mark and bend upward, creating another
    90-degree angle. Repeat at the 4¾" (12cm) mark.

4   With round-nose pliers, create a simple loop at each end
    of the wire at the top of the frame. Place the frame on
    the anvil and hammer evenly, avoiding the loops.

5   Place the 30" (76cm) piece of 26-gauge wire at the top of the frame, just below a loop. Wrap the wire 4 times around 1 side of the frame. Slide a 2mm bead onto the wire and wrap the wire twice around the opposite side of the frame to secure.

6   Continue adding 2mm beads by wrapping the wire around opposite sides of the frame, wrapping twice between each bead or stack. Wrap 7 rows of 1 bead, 6 rows of 2 beads, and 3 rows of 3 beads. Finish and secure by wrapping the wire 3 times around 1 side of the frame. With wire cutters, trim the excess wire. With chain-nose pliers, pinch the wire tightly to the frame.

7   Place the 4" (10cm) piece of 24-gauge wire across the center of the bottom of the frame. Begin wrapping 1 end of the wire 3 times around 1 side of the frame. Slide two 2mm beads, 1 nugget, and 2 more 2mm beads onto the wire. Finish and secure by wrapping the wire 3 times around the other side of the frame. With wire cutters, trim the excess wire. With chain-nose pliers, pinch the wire tightly to the frame.

8   With chain-nose pliers, gently open the top loops by twisting them to the side. Insert the link of chain (or attach a jump ring) into both loops. Close the loops. Attach an ear wire to the link of chain.

9   Repeat steps 1–8 to make the second earring.

Drew earrings, back view.

NICOLE

And the award goes to . . . Nicole Kidman, for
knowing how to seriously rock a pair of earrings on
the red carpet! Over the years I have taken a ton
of inspiration from this woman. She is always so
glamorous, so beautifully accessorized, and so poised.
Earrings appropriate for this Academy Award–
winning actress have to be extra-special, and so the
Nicole earrings take the concept of wrapping stacks of
beads and turn it upside down—literally!

time

50–60 minutes per pair

techniques

looped-back frame (page 28)
looped-ends horseshoe frame (page 29)
wrapping single beads (page 36)
wrapping stacks of beads (page 37)

tools

round-nose pliers
2 pairs of chain-nose pliers
wire cutters
standard and chasing hammers
    (or ball-peen hammer)
anvil
½" (13mm) mandrel
¾" (2cm) mandrel
permanent marker
ruler

materials

17" (43cm) of 18-gauge gold-filled wire
60" (152.5cm) of 26-gauge gold-filled wire
3 links of solid chain or two 6mm jump
    rings
thirty-six 4mm amethyst beads
1 pair of ear wires

finished size

2¼" x 1¾" (5.5cm x 4.5cm)

TO PREP *(for 1 earring)*

Cut two 2" (5cm) pieces of 18-gauge wire,
one 4½" (11.5cm) piece of 18-gauge wire,
one 7" (18cm) piece of 26-gauge wire, one
11" (28cm) piece of 26-gauge wire, and one
12" (30.5cm) piece of 26-gauge wire.
Cut 1 link of solid chain, if using.

TO MAKE

1   To create a variation on the looped-ends horseshoe frame, with round-nose pliers, make an open loop on each end of one of the 2" (5cm) pieces of 18-gauge wire. Place the ½" (13mm) mandrel at the wire's center. (Both looped ends should be facing away from the center of the mandrel.) Gently bend the wire around the mandrel to create the curved top piece of the frame.

2   To create a horseshoe-shaped variation on the looped-back frame, gently bend the other 2" (5cm) piece of 18-gauge wire around the ½" (13mm) mandrel to create the curved center piece of the frame. With round-nose pliers, create loops facing backward at the ends, with the tips of the loops touching the wire frame.

3   Repeat step 2 to create the bottom horseshoe-shaped piece of the frame, using the 4½" (11.5cm) piece of 18-gauge wire and the ¾" (2cm) mandrel. Then, with chain-nose pliers, bend the loops at an approximately 45-degree angle so they stand up straight.

4. Place all 3 pieces of the frame on the anvil and hammer lightly to flatten and texture, being careful to avoid the loops on the middle and bottom pieces of the frame. (a)

5. With the top piece of the frame, place the 7" (18cm) piece of 26-gauge wire next to a loop. Wrap the wire around the frame 4 times. Slide a bead onto the wire to nestle against the inner curve of the frame. Pull the wire flat behind the bead, and secure it by wrapping the wire around the frame twice. (b)

6. Continue adding beads using the technique of wrapping stacks of beads. Add beads in following pattern: 2-1-2. Insert 1 link of solid chain onto the wire (or attach a jump ring) and wrap to the frame (you will attach the ear wire to this link), and continue adding stacks of beads: 4-2-1, keeping layout symmetrical. (Your bead stacks may vary according to the size and shape of your beads.) (c)

   End with 4 wraps, making sure that they are evenly lined up with the other side. With chain-nose pliers, pinch the wire tightly to the frame. With wire cutters, trim the excess wire.

7. With the middle piece of the frame and the 11" (28cm) piece of 26-gauge wire, repeat steps 5 and 6, but add beads in the following pattern and omit the link of chain: 1-1-2-3-4 (center bead stack)-3-2-1-1. The beads should wrap to the bottom of this frame piece. (d)

8. Mark bottom frame 1" below a loop with permanent marker. Place the 12" (30.5cm) piece of wire at the mark, and wrap around the frame 4 times. Slide a bead onto wire to nestle against the outer curve of the frame and wrap the wire 4 times. Continue, adding beads using the technique of wrapping single beads, wrapping the wire 4 times between each bead. Finish and secure by wrapping wire 4 times around the frame. With chain-nose pliers, pinch the wire tightly to the frame. With wire cutters, trim the excess wire. (e)

9. With chain-nose pliers, gently open the loops on the middle frame. Connect these loops to the bottom frame just beneath its loops; *do not* connect the frames loop to loop. With chain-nose pliers, gently open the loops on the bottom frame. Insert these loops through the loops of the top frame piece. Close the loops.

10. With chain-nose pliers, attach an ear wire to the link of chain.

11. Repeat steps 1–10 to make the second earring.

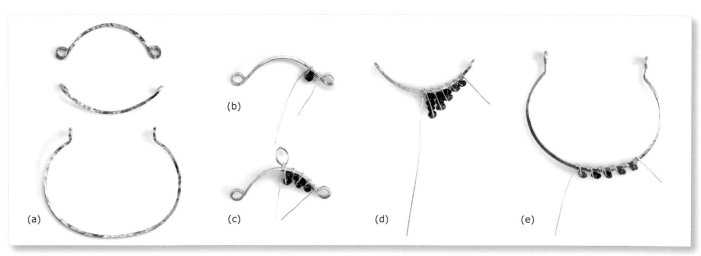

(a) (b) (c) (d) (e)

earrings with intention

The more infatuated I became with gemstones, the more I learned about the layers of value and meaning ascribed to each. For hundreds of years people have used stone beads as symbols and talismans in spiritual and healing matters. It is said that each naturally occurring gemstone has a specific energetic vibration based on the conditions in which the stone was formed, giving it specific metaphysical properties. I am intrigued by this concept and try to apply it to my jewelry making. For example, when a family member falls ill, I make her jewelry using carnelian beads, because carnelian is the stone of healing. When a friend goes through a breakup, I use rose quartz beads, representing emotional balance.

Whether you believe in the power of gemstones to heal or just think that such ideas are all in fun, beads can help us create jewelry with an intention, or purpose. It is my personal philosophy that we can effect change through our actions, even when we're making jewelry. If you have a purpose in your mind while designing—perhaps thinking of the good you wish for your friends—you are reinforcing those thoughts within yourself and creating a beautiful object, sure to communicate your love and care to others. I like to believe that my friends and loved ones will carry the power of my thoughts with them when they wear my jewelry, a physical reminder that will help propel them toward their goals. To me, creating earrings with intention is one small way to make the world a better place. Here are a few of my favorite gemstone beads and their metaphysical properties.

AMETHYST known as the stone of spirituality and dream recall; enhances contentment and meditation and is often used for stress relief

CITRINE brings warmth, joy, and optimism; promotes mental and emotional clarity; dissipates negative energy

LAPIS LAZULI increases knowledge, wisdom, and perfection; attracts wealth and assists in creative expression

PYRITE (FOOL'S GOLD) shields the wearer from negative energy and enhances intellect and memory; often symbolizes the sun

ROSE QUARTZ represents love, beauty, peacefulness, and emotional balance; facilitates emotional healing, calms stress, relieves hurt, and dissolves fear

RUBY promotes loving, nurturing thoughts and actions, and attracts wealth and protection; helps to amplify energy, both positive and negative

SAPPHIRE increases joy, beauty, and prosperity

TOURMALINE enhances inspiration, understanding, and self-confidence (A great stone to wear while making earrings!)

ALI

Day or night, work or play, the Ali earrings
are your go-to earrings for subtle glamour and
sparkle. They have proved so popular that I
design a new color palette for them each season.
One of the smaller earrings in the Double
Happiness Jewelry collection, Ali earrings can
easily be adjusted to any size you prefer. Just
choose a larger or smaller mandrel when making
the teardrop looped-back frame. When making
variations of these earrings, I suggest that you
take notes on wire dimension as well as bead
count, so that when your friends go crazy over
your new earrings, you can make pairs for them
in a flash!

time

20–30 minutes per pair

techniques

looped-back frame (page 28)
wrapping stacks of beads (page 37)

tools

round-nose pliers
2 pairs of chain-nose pliers
wire cutters
¾" (2cm) mandrel
standard hammer
anvil
ruler

materials

8" (20.5cm) of 18-gauge gold-filled wire
24" (61cm) of 26-gauge gold-filled wire
3 links of solid chain or two 6mm jump rings
forty-four 3mm gold metal faceted beads
1 pair of ear wires

finished size

2" x 1" (5cm x 2.5cm)

TO PREP *(for 1 earring)*

Cut one 4" (10cm) piece of 18-gauge wire and one 12" (30.5cm) piece of 26-gauge wire.
Cut 1 link of solid chain, if using.

TO MAKE

1 Create a looped-back frame in a teardrop shape using the ¾" (2cm) mandrel and the 4" (10cm) piece of 18-gauge wire.

2 With chain-nose pliers, carefully open the loops and insert 1 link of chain (or attach a jump ring). Return the loops to their original positions to secure.

3 Place the 12" (30.5cm) piece of 26-gauge wire just below the center of the left side of frame, about 1" (2.5cm) from the top of the frame. Wrap the wire around the frame 5 times, making sure to wrap the wire while holding the frame right side up, so the wire will be hidden behind the beads as you wrap. Slide one 3mm bead onto the wire and grip it against the frame with your fingers. Pull the wire down behind the bead, tightly wrapping twice around the frame.

4 Continue adding beads using the technique of wrapping stacks of beads to a frame. Add beads in the following pattern: 1-1-2-1-3-4 (center bead stack)-3-1-2-1-1, keeping the layout symmetrical. End with 5 wraps, making sure that it is evenly lined up with the other side. With chain-nose pliers, pinch the wire tightly to the frame. With wire cutters, trim the excess wire.

5 With chain-nose pliers, attach an ear wire to the chain link.

6 Repeat steps 1–5 to make the second earring.

SOLACE

I've made these Solace earrings using white agate for a glamorous, super-clean, monochromatic palette sure to gleam brightly in a dark room or club. But they can be made so many different ways. Their two layers double the color design possibilities, so have fun mixing and matching beads. You're sure to find a color combination perfect for any occasion.

time

30–45 minutes per pair

techniques

looped-back frame (page 28)
wrapping stacks of beads (page 37)

tools

round-nose pliers
2 pairs of chain-nose pliers
wire cutters
½" (13mm) mandrel
¾" (2cm) mandrel
ruler

materials

19" (48.5cm) of 18-gauge gold-filled wire
68" (172.5cm) of 26-gauge gold-filled
    wire
seventy 3mm faceted white agate beads
3 links of rectangle chain or two 7mm
    jump rings
1 pair of ear wires

finished size

2¾" x 1½" (7cm x 3.8cm)

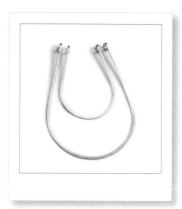

TO PREP *(for 1 earring)*

Cut one 5¾" (14.5cm) piece of 18-gauge wire, one
3¾" (9.5cm) piece of 18-gauge wire, one 18"
(45.5cm) piece of 26-gauge wire, one 12" (30.5cm)
piece of 26-gauge wire, and two 2" (5cm) pieces of
26-gauge wire.
Cut 1 link of chain, if using.

TO MAKE

1   Create a looped-back frame in a teardrop shape using
the ½" (13mm) mandrel and the 5¾" (14.5cm) piece
of 18-gauge wire. Repeat this step using the ¾" (2cm)
mandrel and the 3¾" (9.5cm) piece of 18-gauge wire.

2   With the larger teardrop frame, place the 18" (45.5cm)
piece of 26-gauge wire about ⅓ from the bottom of the
frame. Wrap the wire around the frame 5 times. Slide a
bead onto the wire to nestle against the inner curve of
the frame. Pull the wire flat behind the bead, and secure
it by wrapping the wire around the frame twice, making
sure to wrap the wire while holding the frame right side
up, so the wire will be hidden behind the beads as you
wrap.

3   Continue adding beads using the technique of wrapping
stacks of beads to a frame, wrapping twice between each
bead stack. Add beads in the following pattern: 2-3-
4-5 (center stack)-4-3-2. (Your bead stacks may vary
according to the size and shape of your beads.) Finish
and secure by wrapping wire 5 times around the frame.
With chain-nose pliers, pinch the wire tightly to the
frame. With wire cutters, trim the excess wire.

4   With the smaller teardrop frame, place the 12" (30.5cm) piece of 26-gauge wire about halfway from the bottom of the frame. Wrap the wire around the frame 5 times, as in step 3. Add beads in the following pattern: 2-2-3 (center stack)-2-2. Finish and secure by wrapping wire 5 times around the frame. With chain-nose pliers, pinch the wire tightly to the frame. With wire cutters, trim the excess wire.

5   With chain-nose pliers, gently open both loops on the smaller teardrop frame. Insert 1 link of rectangle chain onto both loops (or attach a jump ring). Close loops to secure.

6   With chain-nose pliers, gently open both loops on the larger teardrop frame. Hook the loops onto the link of chain on each side of the smaller teardrop frame. Close the loops to secure.

7   Take one 2" (5cm) piece of 26-gauge wire and begin wrapping 7 times around both frames just below a set of loops. With chain-nose pliers, pinch the wire tightly to the frame. With wire cutters, trim the excess wire.

Repeat on the other side of the frames with the remaining 2" (5cm) piece of 26-gauge wire.

8   With chain-nose pliers, attach an ear wire to the link of chain.

9   Repeat steps 1–8 to make the second earring.

REESE

For East-meets-West glamour, reach for Reese earrings. I love the way the wires gracefully descend toward the center, calling attention to the bead clusters at the top and bottom of the frame. This design adds wire embellishments and bead-cluster dangles to a simple crossover loop-and-lock teardrop frame for an impressive look that will keep your days cool and your nights hot.

time

45–60 minutes per pair

techniques

crossover loop-and-lock teardrop frame
  (page 31)
single wrapped loop (page 33)
eye pin (page 38)
bead cluster drops (page 75)

tools

round-nose pliers
2 pairs of chain-nose pliers
wire cutters
½" (13mm) mandrel
standard hammer
anvil
ruler

materials

11" (28cm) of 16-gauge sterling silver wire
36" (91cm) of 20-gauge sterling silver wire
32" (81cm) of 24-gauge sterling silver wire
sixteen 4mm metal faceted beads
7 links of common chain or four 4.5mm jump rings
1 pair of ear wires

finished size

2¾" x 1¼" (7cm x 3cm)

TO PREP *(for 1 earring)*

Cut one 5½" (14cm) piece of 16-gauge
wire, two 4" (10cm) pieces of
20-gauge wire, two 5" (12.5cm)
pieces of 20-gauge wire, and eight
2" (5cm) pieces of 24-gauge wire.

Cut two 1-link pieces of chain, if using.

TO MAKE

1 Create a crossover loop-and-lock teardrop frame using
   the ½" (13mm) mandrel and the 5½" (14cm) piece of
   16-gauge wire. (a)

2 Place one 4" (10cm) piece of 20-gauge wire against
   the back side of the frame about ⅓ from the bottom.
   (A short tail should extend away from the center of the
   frame.) Wrap the long end of the wire around the frame
   3 times. (This tail should now extend over the front of
   the frame toward the center.) With your thumb, curve
   this wire tail and create a slight U shape in the wire,
   bending toward the center of the frame. Secure this
   U shape in place by wrapping the wire approximately
   ½" (13mm) from the center bottom of the frame with
   2 wraps toward the center of the frame. (The long tail
   should now be at the back of the frame.)

   Bring this same piece of wire back up and wrap it 3
   times to secure above the first 3 wraps, making sure this
   end aligns between the wire just placed and the frame,
   again curving the wire with your thumb to match the
   first curve. With wire cutters, trim the excess wire. With
   chain-nose pliers, pinch the wire tightly to the frame. (b)

3 Repeat step 2 with a 5" (12.5cm) piece of 20-gauge
   wire, beginning by placing the wire above the second
   wrap created in step 2 and making sure to space each
   set of wraps evenly (about ⅛" [3mm] apart). Match the
   curves of the wire as you work. (c)

4   Repeat steps 2–3 on the other side of the frame.

5   With round-nose pliers, make an eye pin with one 2"
    (5cm) piece of 24-gauge wire. Slide on a bead and finish
    with a single wrapped loop. Repeat 5 times, creating 6
    bead dangles.

6   Create a bead cluster drop with a 2" (5cm) piece of
    24-gauge wire: Begin a wrapped loop but *before closing
    the loop*, insert 3 bead dangles created in step 5. Wrap to
    close, then slide on a bead. Begin the final wrapped loop
    but *before closing the loop*, hook this open loop onto the
    bottom of the frame. Wrap to close. With wire cutters,
    trim the excess wire.

7   Create another bead cluster drop with another 2" (5cm)
    piece of 24-gauge wire: Begin a wrapped loop but *before
    closing the loop*, insert the remaining 3 bead dangles
    created in step 5. Wrap to close, then slide on a bead.
    Begin the final wrapped loop, but *before closing the loop*,
    insert 1 link of chain (or attach a jump ring). Wrap to
    close. With wire cutters, trim the excess wire.

8   With chain-nose pliers, open up the bottom loop of the
    frame and insert the link of chain attached to the
    bead cluster drop made in step 7. Close the loop to lock
    and secure.

9   With chain-nose pliers, gently open the top loop of the
    frame and insert 1 link of common chain (or attach a
    jump ring). Wrap to close. Attach an ear wire to the link
    of chain.

10 Repeat steps 1–9 to make the second earring.

    Note: It helps to maintain an image of this earring in front of
    you as you work on it. The design is organic in nature, and
    "eyeballing" it to help you judge the correct wire placement will
    be important. When creating the decorative wire wraps, begin
    with the lowest point on the side of the frame.

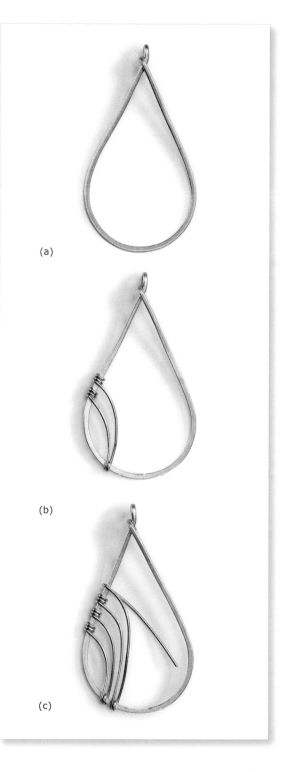

(a)

(b)

(c)

Chapter 6

R ock and roll has always pushed the boundaries—at times demanding, sexy, dark, and even messy—but it's always completely cool, just like the women who rock out like no one else can!

In this chapter you can't help but notice the bold, daring, and edgy looks that scream, "Look at me!" You will explore some new techniques with different materials, such as fabric and thread, and make earrings worn by rock-and-roll celebrities such as Alicia Keys and Britney Spears. Finally, you will learn about chain and chain lengths, creating the illusion of length through the neck.

ROCK AND ROLL

So put on some Zeppelin, bust out your tools, make yourself a pair of rocker-chic earrings, and rock on! These earrings won't just bring out your inner groupie; they'll get you up on the stage.

"In this chapter you will explore new techniques and make earrings worn by rock-and-roll celebrities."

Go as wild as you want—leather, chain, zebra print—these simple hoops complement the wildest combination in your closet. Seriously, who does not love to wear hoops? The simplicity of this design flatters any face and can be made as dramatic or laid-back as you like. The Priscilla earrings are instantly adaptable. I used pyrite—my latest obsession—to create the bead dangle shown here, but you can slide on any bead dangle to instantly match this earring to your night out. After you learn this basic design, you may also want to experiment with different mandrel sizes to change the hoop size.

So have fun with this hoop. Make a pair for yourself and another for a friend—it's fun and easy, and everyone who wears them will feel

PRISCILLA

time

5–10 minutes per pair

techniques

*crossover loop-and-lock hoop frame
    (page 30)*
simple loop (page 32)
single wrapped loop (page 33)
eye pin (page 38)

tools

round-nose pliers
2 pairs of chain-nose pliers
wire cutters
1¼" (3cm) mandrel
standard hammer
anvil
ruler

materials

14" (35.5cm) of 16-gauge gold-filled wire
4" (10cm) of 24-gauge gold-filled wire
two 6mm pyrite nugget beads
*3 links of common chain or two 4.5mm jump
    rings*
1 pair of ear wires

finished size

2¾" x 1¾" (7cm x 4.5cm)

TO PREP *(for 1 earring)*

Cut one 7" (18cm) piece of 16-gauge wire and
  one 2" (5cm) piece of 24-gauge wire.
Cut 1 link of common chain, if using.

TO MAKE

1   Create an eye pin from the 2" (5cm) piece of 24-gauge
    wire. Slide a bead onto the eye pin and close with a single
    wrapped loop, making sure the circumference of the
    wrapped loop will fit over the 16-gauge wire. With wire
    cutters, trim the excess wire.

2   Create a crossover loop-and-lock hoop frame using the
    1¼" (3cm) mandrel and the 7" (15cm) piece of 16-gauge
    wire, but *before closing the frame loop*, insert the bead
    dangle created in step 1. Close the hoop frame to finish
    and secure.

3   With chain-nose pliers, open the simple loop atop the
    hoop and insert 1 link of chain (or attach a jump ring).
    Attach an ear wire to the link of chain.

4   Repeat steps 1–3 to make the second earring.

SCARLETT

Bold, beautiful, dramatic, and noticeable, the
Scarlett earrings make me want to pull my hair
back, put on a sexy evening dress and red lipstick,
and go dancing. The Scarlett earrings will shimmy
and shake right along with you—the weight of the
beads and the flexibility of the chain allow for a lot
of swing when you move. In addition, the frame
shape and drape of the chain work together to
create a plunging V formation. The size, shape,
and swing of the earrings will definitely bring
attention your way.

time
15–20 minutes per pair

techniques
simple loop (page 32)
single wrapped loop (page 33)
eye pin (page 38)

tools
round-nose pliers
2 pairs of chain-nose pliers
wire cutters
mandrel
standard hammer
anvil
permanent marker
ruler

materials
7" (18cm) of 16-gauge gold-filled wire
12" (30.5cm) of 24-gauge gold-filled wire
six 5mm red coral coin-shaped beads
267 links of dainty chain
1 pair ear wires

finished size
4¼" x 2" (11cm x 5cm)

TO PREP *(for 1 earring)*

Cut one 3½" (9cm) piece of 16-gauge wire
and mark it in the center at 1¾" (4.5cm)
with a permanent marker.
Cut three 2" (5cm) pieces of 24-gauge wire.
Cut one 23-link piece, one 41-link piece, and
one 67-link piece of chain.

TO MAKE

1 To create the support, grasp the 3½" (9cm) piece of wire
at the mark with round-nose pliers and wrap the wire
around the widest part of the top jaw of the pliers. Cross
the wire ends to create a loop in the center. With round-
nose pliers, create simple loops on each end, facing up,
in the same direction as the center loop.

2 Place the support on the anvil and gently hammer the
entire piece of wire to flatten, including the loops.

3 Create an eye pin from one 2" (5cm) piece of 24-gauge
wire. Slide on a bead and begin a single wrapped loop,
but *do not* close the loop. Repeat to create 3 bead
dangles. Attach 1 wrapped bead dangle to the center link
of each chain. Wrap to close the loops. With wire cutters,
trim the excess wire.

4 With chain-nose pliers, gently open both side loops of
the support by twisting them to the side. Insert 1 end
link of each chain onto 1 open loop in order of shortest
to longest. Close the loop. Insert the opposite ends of
each chain onto other open loop in order of shortest to
longest. Close the loop.

5 With chain-nose pliers, attach an ear wire to the center
loop of the support.

6 Repeat steps 1–5 to make the second earring.

BEYONCÉ

Beyoncé—a woman after my own heart—knows how to seriously rock out (and also how to rock Double Happiness earrings and necklaces, on many occasions). She was once interviewed about her status as a sex symbol. She replied, "I like to dress sexy, and I carry myself like a lady." *I love that!* To me, dressing sexy is about wearing a few pieces that get attention, and that gets respect. And there is no accessory that says, "Notice me, I am a woman and I am bold, but I am a lady and I respect myself," like the Beyoncé earrings.

time
50–60 minutes per pair

techniques
simple loop (page 32)
single wrapped loop (page 33)
eye pin (page 35)

tools
round-nose pliers
2 pairs of chain-nose pliers
wire cutters
standard hammer
anvil
permanent marker
ruler

materials
14" (35.5cm) of 16-gauge gold-filled wire
20" (51cm) of 24-gauge gold-filled wire
80" (203cm) of 26-gauge gold-filled wire
ten 8mm coin pearl beads
3 links of solid chain or two 6mm jump rings
1 pair of ear wires

finished size
3½" x 2½" (9cm x 6.5cm)

TO PREP *(for 1 earring)*

Cut one 7" (18cm) piece of 16-gauge wire and mark the wire at 2", 3½", and 5" (5cm, 9cm, and 12.5cm) with the permanent marker.

Cut five 2" (5cm) pieces of 24-gauge wire and one 40" (101.5cm) piece of 26-gauge wire.

Cut 1 link of solid chain, if using.

TO MAKE

1   Create an eye pin from 1 piece of 2" (5cm) 24-gauge wire. Slide on a pearl. Wrap to close. Repeat 4 times to make 5 dangles.

2   With chain-nose pliers, grasp the 7" (18cm) piece of 16-gauge wire at the 3½" mark and bend the wire up at a 45-degree angle to create a V shape. Repeat at the 5" (12.5cm) mark and the 2" (5cm) mark, creating a diamond-shaped frame.

3   With round-nose pliers, create a simple loop on each top side of the frame, looping back both ends of the wire in the same direction. Place the wire on the anvil and hammer to flatten, avoiding the loops.

Gently open 1 loop by twisting it to the side and insert a chain link (or attach a jump ring). Close the loop. Gently open the other loop by twisting it to the side and insert the same link to hold the frame together. Close the loop.

4   Begin wrapping the 40" (101.5cm) piece of 26-gauge wire around the frame, starting about ¼" (6mm) above a side bend of the frame. Wrap approximately 13 times to the corner point. Slide a bead dangle created in step 1 onto the wire. Wrap the dangle to the frame and continue wrapping down the side to about halfway between the corners (approximately 42 times). Slide another bead dangle onto the wire. Continue wrapping the wire down the side of the frame until you reach the bottom corner of the frame.

Slide a bead dangle onto the wire and begin wrapping the wire up the opposite side of the frame, repeating the pattern of wraps and bead dangles to match the other side of the frame. After attaching the last bead dangle, secure by wrapping the wire 13 times around the frame. With wire cutters, trim the excess wire. With chain-nose pliers, pinch the wire tightly to the frame.

5   With chain-nose pliers, attach an ear wire to the chain link.

6   Repeat steps 1–5 to make the second earring.

BRITNEY

Britney Spears was spied on a shopping trip
in Los Angeles wearing a pink-pearl version of
this earring—as a necklace! Whether you love
her music or prefer heavy metal, you've got to
give props to Britney for such a creative way to
accessorize.

This book is devoted to earrings, but keep your
mind open about all the ways you can apply
the techniques in this book. Who says you can't
take an earring, slide it onto a chain, and
make it a necklace? Hey Brit, thanks for
showing us that sometimes an earring can be
so much more!

time

25–30 minutes per pair

techniques

simple loop (page 32)
wrapping stacks of beads (page 37)

tools

round-nose pliers
2 pairs of chain-nose pliers
wire cutters
standard hammer
anvil
½" (13mm) mandrel
permanent marker
ruler

materials

14" (35.5cm) of 16-gauge gold-filled wire
8" (20.5cm) of 22-gauge gold-filled wire
32" (81cm) of 26-gauge gold-filled wire
thirty-eight 4mm azurite beads
3 links of common chain or two 4.5mm jump
  rings
1 pair of ear wires

finished size

2¾" x 1" (7cm x 2.5cm)

Note: If you would like for your earrings to be mirror images, as shown, rather than matching, reverse the bead order in step 7 when making the second earring.

TO PREP *(for 1 earring)*

Cut one 7" (18cm) piece of 16-gauge wire, one 4" (10cm) piece of 22-gauge wire, and one 16" (40.5cm) piece of 26-gauge wire.
Cut 1 link of common chain, if using.

TO MAKE

1   Straighten the 7" (18cm) piece of 16-gauge wire by running it through your fingers. Place the wire on the anvil and hammer to flatten.

2   Remove the wire from the anvil and mark it at the center (3½" [9cm]) with the permanent marker. With chain-nose pliers, grasp the flat sides of the wire at the mark. With your fingers, bend both sides up to create a V shape.

3   Place the ½" (13mm) mandrel in the center of the V. With your fingers, lightly bend the wire around the mandrel to create a leaf shape.

4   With round-nose pliers, gently create a simple loop, bending 1 tail-end of the wire back toward itself, touching the back of earring.

5   With the 4" (10cm) piece of 22-gauge wire, wrap both ends of the frame together tightly, just below the loop. With wire cutters, trim the excess wire at the top of the frame that has not been looped, cutting as close to the wire wraps as possible.

6   Place the 16" (40.5cm) piece of 26-gauge wire about halfway up one side of the frame. Wrap the wire 7 times, working toward the base of the leaf shape.

7   Slide 1 bead onto the wire to nestle against the inside of the frame. Grip the bead with your fingers and pull the wire flat behind the bead, tightly wrapping twice around the frame. Continue adding beads using the technique of wrapping stacks of beads to a frame. Add beads in the following pattern: 2-2-2-1-1 (center stack)-1-2-2-2-2-1. Finish and secure by wrapping the wire 7 times, making sure that it evenly aligns with the other side. With chain-nose pliers, pinch the wire tightly to the frame. With wire cutters, trim the excess wire.

8   With chain-nose pliers, gently open the top loop of the frame and insert 1 link of chain (or attach a jump ring). Attach an ear wire to this link.

9   Repeat steps 1–8 to make the second earring.

Britney earrings, side view (top) and back view (above).

Your Perfect Match!
Finding the Right Metal for Your Skin Tone

Ever wonder which type of metal is perfect for you? By using skin-tone color matching, or color analysis, you can help determine which metal will best show off your skin. All skin tones fall into two categories, "cool" or "warm." Cool skin tones have pink or blue undertones (think Nicole Kidman). Warm skin tones have yellow or green undertones (think Halle Berry).

Take a look at your skin's undertones, and refer to the table below to determine which metal is your perfect match.

SKINTONE	CELEBRITY	BEST METAL TO WEAR
Fair, Cool	Nicole Kidman	Sterling Silver
Medium-Fair, Warm	Jennifer Aniston	Gold, Bronze, Copper
Medium-Dark, Warm	Jennifer Lopez	Gold, Bronze
Dark, Cool	Alek Wek	Sterling Silver

Clockwise: Model Alek Wek, singer Jennifer Lopez, and actor Jennifer Aniston.

MADONNA

Lose five pounds instantly with these ultra-hip rock-and-roll earrings! Just kidding—you won't really lose five pounds, but it's no joke that you will look like you have a thinner, longer neck!

Named after the undisputed queen of keeping fit, the Madonna earrings are sure to bring out the long and lean in you. Wear the long fringe next to the face to create an optical illusion that lengthens the neck. You may not have lost five pounds, but these earrings will make you feel like you did!

Note: If you would like your earrings to be mirror images, as shown, rather than matching, flip the second earring frame before attaching the ear wire.

time
70–80 minutes per pair

techniques
simple loop (page 32)
single wrapped loop (page 33)
double wrapped loop (page 34)
eye pin (page 38)

tools
round-nose pliers
2 pairs of chain-nose pliers
wire cutters
standard hammer
anvil
ruler

materials
5" (12.5cm) of 16-gauge gold-filled wire
4" (10cm) of 24-gauge gold-filled wire
32" (61cm) of 26-gauge gold-filled wire
thirty-two 3–4mm watermelon tourmaline beads
66 links of common chain (about 10" [25.5cm])
430 links of dainty chain
1 pair of ear wires

finished size
5" x 1½" (12.5cm x 3.8cm)

TO PREP *(for 1 earring)*

Cut one 2½" (6.5cm) piece of 16-gauge wire,
    one 2" (5cm) piece of 24-gauge wire, one 10"
    (25.5) piece of 26-gauge wire, and sixteen 2"
    (5cm) pieces of 26-gauge wire.
Cut one 21-link piece and one 10-link piece of
    common chain.
Cut 1 piece each of dainty chain in the following
    lengths: 20, 19, 18, 17, 16, 15, 14, 13, 12,
    11, 10, 9, 8, 7, 6, and 5 links.
Select 16 beads and organize from light to dark
    to create an ombré effect.

TO MAKE

1   To create the center bar support, with
    round-nose pliers, create simple loops
    on both ends of the 2½" (6.5cm) piece
    of 16-gauge wire. The loops should
    curve under, toward the center of the
    wire. Place the frame on the anvil and
    hammer lightly until flat.

2   Create an eye pin from a 2" (5cm)
    piece of 26-gauge wire. Slide a bead
    onto the eye pin and begin a single wrapped loop, but *before
    closing the loop*, insert 1 end of a piece of dainty chain. Wrap
    to close. Repeat 15 times so that all 16 pieces of cut dainty
    chain have a single bead attached.

3   Place the 10" (25.5cm) piece of 26-gauge wire at the base of
    a loop on the bar support and wrap it 4 times tightly around
    the bar support.

4   Slide the longest piece of dainty chain onto the wire and
    wrap the wire twice around the bar support. Continue adding
    chain dangles from longest to shortest until you reach the
    end of the bar support, attaching all 16 dangles with 2 wraps
    between each dangle. Finish and secure by wrapping the wire
    4 times around the bar support at the base of the opposite
    loop. With wire cutters, trim the excess wire. With chain-nose
    pliers, pinch the wire tightly to the bar support.

5   With chain-nose pliers, gently open the loop on the bar
    support next to the shortest chain dangle by twisting it.
    Insert 1 end of the 10-link piece of common chain. Close the
    loop. Gently open the opposite loop of the bar support and
    insert 1 end of the 21-link piece of common chain. Close the
    loop.

6   Begin a double wrapped loop with the 2" (5cm) piece of
    24-gauge wire, but *before closing the loop*, insert both ends
    of common chain onto the open loop. Wrap to close. Make
    the final wrapped loop. Attach an ear wire to the top wrapped
    loop.

7   Repeat steps 1–6 to make the second earring.

OSIRIS

What is it about serpent jewelry that is so compelling, appealing, and chic? In early mythology, serpents were symbols of energy and life. Ancient African societies saw the serpents as symbols of fertility. Carl Jung said the serpent represents the unconscious mind. Personally, I just feel sexy when I wear them. (And I'm not the only one. Alicia Keys, Carrie Underwood, and Katharine McPhee also wear these earrings.) Whatever your interpretation—energy, fertility, the unconscious mind, or just super-hip style—the sinewy nature of curves in this design will make you feel sexy and cool.

time
50–60 minutes per pair

techniques
simple loop (page 32)
teardrop loop and wrap (page 35)
wrapping single beads (page 36)

tools
round-nose pliers
2 pairs of chain-nose pliers
wire cutters
ballpoint pen or similar-width mandrel
¼" (6mm) mandrel
permanent marker
standard hammer
anvil
ruler

materials
14" (35.5cm) of 16-gauge gold-filled wire
4" (10cm) of 24-gauge gold-filled wire
4' (2.4m) of 26-gauge gold-filled wire
forty-six 4mm faceted round black onyx
    beads
two 4mm x 6mm black onyx briolettes
5 links of common chain
1 pair of ear wires

finished size
1½" x 1½" (3.8cm x 3.8cm)

TO PREP *(for 1 earring)*

Cut one 7" (18cm) piece of 16-gauge wire, one
    2" (5cm) piece of 24-gauge wire, and one 2'
    (1.2m) piece of 26-gauge wire.
Cut one 2-link piece of chain.

TO MAKE

1   With round-nose pliers, create simple loops on each end
    of the 7" (18cm) piece of 16-gauge wire. Mark the frame
    with the permanent marker, measuring from 1 loop to
    ¾", 2¼", 4", and 5¼" (2cm, 5.5cm, 10cm, 14.5cm).

2   Place the ballpoint pen (or similar-width mandrel) at the
    ¾" (2cm) mark and use it as a mandrel to bend the wire.
    Place the ¼" (6mm) mandrel at the 2¼" (5.5cm) mark
    and bend the wire around it in the opposite direction,
    creating an S shape. (This frame is a series of S turns.)
    Place the ballpoint pen at 4" (10cm) and bend the wire
    around it, again in the opposite direction, and repeat at
    the 5¼" (14.5cm) mark. Place the frame on the anvil and
    hammer lightly, avoiding the loops on each end. (a, b, c)

3   Wrap one 4' (1.2m) piece of 26-gauge wire 7 times
    around the frame next to the top loop. (d)

Note: If you would like your earrings to be mirror images, as shown,
rather than matching, flip frame when attaching the ear wire for the
second earring.

4   Slide on 1 round bead to nestle against the inside curve of the frame and wrap the wire 7 times. Continue adding beads using the technique of wrapping beads to a frame until you reach the end of the frame (about 23 beads), wrapping the wire 7 times between each bead. Finish and secure the wire by wrapping it 7 times around the frame. With wire cutters, trim the excess wire. With chain-nose pliers, pinch the wire tightly to the frame. (e, f)

5   With the 2" (5cm) piece of 24-gauge wire, form a teardrop loop and wrap around a briolette. With wire cutters, trim the excess wire. With chain-nose pliers, gently open the bottom loop of the frame by twisting it to the side. Insert the briolette loop and wrap. Close the loop.

6   With chain-nose pliers, open the top loop of the frame. Insert the 2-link piece of chain. Close the loop. Attach an ear wire to the top chain link.

7   Repeat steps 1–6 to make the second earring.

wrap it up

When you work with designs that require a long wire tail to wrap beads to the frame (like the Osiris earrings), managing the tail can be challenging. You don't want the wire to kink or twist while you work. I find that the process of wrapping is more manageable when I add the beads on one at a time. I don't have to worry about all those beads slipping off, and can manipulate the direction of the frame any way I like. But some of the women who work with me like to string all the beads on in the beginning and then isolate each bead as they wrap. They find that this method allows them to get into a wrapping rhythm, like a meditative trance, and that pausing to add beads takes them out of it. However you choose to add beads, the result will be gorgeous!

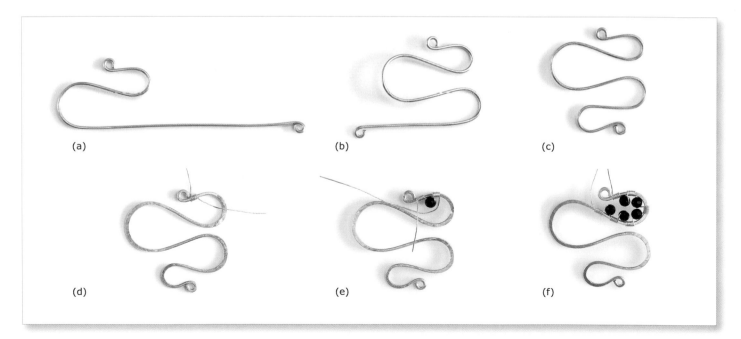

(a)   (b)   (c)

(d)   (e)   (f)

STEVIE

A tribute to one of the greatest female rockers ever: Stevie Nicks. These earrings are so Stevie circa 1970! Make them big or small, add other bead styles, and make them in any color (or every color) for lightweight earrings that will suit your style perfectly!

Give yourself some time to get used to this technique. For these and the Fergie earrings on page 150, you will be carefully using glue to keep the silk threads in place. This is a skill unto itself, so I suggest a few trials runs of wrapping and gluing.

time
45–60 minutes per pair

technique
simple loop (page 32)

tools
round-nose pliers
2 chain-nose pliers
wire cutters
standard hammer
anvil
permanent marker
1" (2.5cm) mandrel
ruler
scissors

materials
29" (74cm) of 18-gauge craft wire
18" (45.5cm) of 24-gauge gold-filled wire
ten 4mm brass rectangle beads
30' (9.1m) of silk embroidery thread
instant glue
1 pair of ear wires

finished size
2½" x 2" (6.5cm x 5cm)

Note: The circumference of the precut bottom ring of the ear wire must be large enough to accommodate the 18-gauge wire frame.

TO PREP *(for 1 earring)*

Cut one 14½" (37cm) piece of 18-gauge wire and mark it at 7¼" (18.5cm) with the permanent marker.
Cut three 3" (7.5cm) pieces of 24-gauge wire.
Cut 15' (4.6m) of embroidery thread.

TO MAKE

1 With round-nose pliers, grasp the 14½" (37cm) piece of 18-gauge wire at the 7¼" mark. Wrap the wire around one jaw of the round-nose pliers to create the top loop. (This will be called end A.) (a)

2 Lay the frame on the table. (It should be shaped like a long V with the loop on 1 end and 2 wire edges at the other.) With the permanent marker, mark the frame 1¼" (3cm) from both tail-ends.

3 With chain-nose pliers, grasp both tail-ends of the frame together near the marks. Wrap 1 tail-end wire around the other tail-end at the mark 3 times. With wire cutters, trim the excess wire from the wrap. Lightly hammer the frame. (b)

4 With wire cutters, trim the end of the wire to ¾" (2cm). With round-nose pliers, create a simple loop. (This will be called end B.) (c)

5 With the permanent marker, mark the wire at ¾", 1½", and 2¼" (2cm, 3.8cm, and 5.5cm) from end A. (These are the locations where you will wrap beads to the frame.)

6 Lay the marked frame on your work surface; the side facing you will become the front of the frame. Center one 3" (7.5cm) piece of 24-gauge wire across the back of the frame at the ¾" (2cm) mark, so that each tail-end extending beyond the sides of the frame is the same length (approximately 1¼" [3cm]). Wrap the right-side tail 3 times around the right side of the frame.

7   Bring the tail-end across the back side of the frame to the other side of the long wire. Slide on a bead. Bring the tail-end to the left side of the frame and wrap 3 times. On the back of the frame, cross it to the other side of the center beaded wire and wrap the other side 3 times. With wire cutters, trim the excess wire. With chain-nose pliers, pinch the wire tightly to the frame. (d)

8   Repeat the process in steps 6–7 at the 1¼" (3cm) and 2¼" (5.5cm) marks, using 2 beads at each mark.

9   Attach the embroidery thread to the top of the frame (end A) by tying it directly below the loop. Hold the short tail against 1 side of the frame and carefully apply 1 drop of glue at the knots on the frame above the first bead.

10 Begin to wrap the long end of the embroidery thread and around and down the frame toward the first bead, over the thread tail. When you reach the first bead, cross the embroidery thread behind the bead and continue to wrap. *Do not* wrap the embroidery silk over the wire that holds the bead in place. (e)

11 Carefully apply glue to the frame above the second set of beads and continue to wrap, crossing the thread behind the beads. *Do not* wrap the embroidery thread over the wire that holds the beads in place. Continue to apply glue to the frame above the beads and wrap, crossing the embroidery thread behind the beads, until you reach the end of the frame (end B). (f)

12 Knot the thread to 1 side, directly below the loop. Carefully apply a dot of glue to the knot. With scissors, trim the thread.

13 Wrap the entire frame around the 1" (2.5cm) mandrel. With chain-nose pliers, gently open end B by twisting the loop. With your nondominant hand, carefully squeeze the frame ends together and hook end A in the open loop. Close the loop. With chain-nose pliers, attach an ear wire to the loop you just closed.

14 Repeat steps 1–13 to make the second earring.

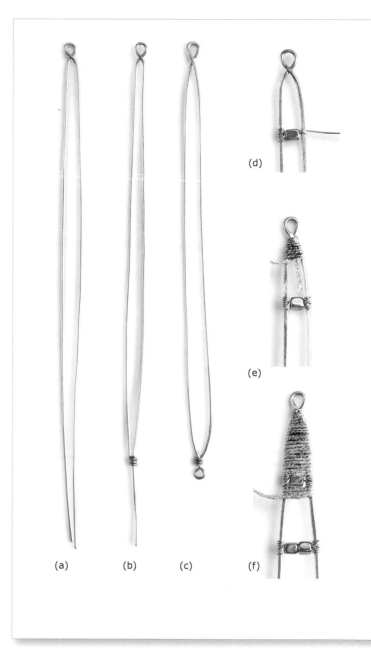

(a)   (b)   (c)   (f)

(d)

(e)

Note: Don't use expensive sterling silver or gold-filled wire for the frame of the Stevie earrings. You can use inexpensive craft wire, as your silk thread will be covering it. Just make sure the wire gauge is the same as recommended in the materials list (otherwise, your earrings will be fragile).

FERGIE

Ah, the life of a rock star. Sleep all day, rock
and roll all night. Traveling from town to town,
always a new city on the horizon. Thousands of
fans screaming your name! Exciting, sure—but
being fabulous is hard work, too. Fortunately,
the Fergie earrings make accessorizing easy.

The design for these earrings took me a looooong
time to figure out. Like the Stevie earrings (page
147), you will have to build the wire frame first
and then wrap it with silk thread to create this
hard-partying look. It's definitely a cool style,
but it will require patience until you learn
the pattern and become adept at gluing.
Do you have it in you to be a rock star?
Even if you don't have the lifestyle, you
can still look the part!

SHAKIRA

Shakira knows how to make things move! These earrings are an ode to an amazing singer, an innovative dancer, and a great humanitarian. When Shakira is not performing, she is helping those in need, providing support to children who have been displaced by violence and are living in poverty.

When these earrings were part of the Double Happiness Jewelry collection, a portion of the proceeds were donated to a local foster home called The Polinsky Children's Center. In addition to helping the center financially, we work with the kids there to help them create beautiful jewelry of their own. I hope that the day you make these earrings, and the days you wear them, you will both embody and experience what they mean to me: consciousness, kindness, and generosity.

time
50–60 minutes per pair

techniques
looped-ends horseshoe frame (page 29)
simple loop (page 32)
wrapping single beads (page 36)

tools
round-nose pliers
2 pairs of chain-nose pliers
wire cutters
½" (13mm) mandrel
¾" (2cm) mandrel
1" (2.5cm) mandrel
standard hammer
anvil
ruler

materials
13" (33cm) of 16-gauge gold-filled wire
9' (2.7m) of 26-gauge gold-filled wire
ten 3mm faceted garnet rondelles
fourteen 3mm faceted labrodorite rondelles
twenty-four 3mm faceted carnelian rondelles
43 links of sturdy chain
1 pair of ear wires

finished size
2" x 2" (5cm x 5cm)

TO PREP *(for 1 earring)*

Cut one 1½" (3.8cm) piece of 16-gauge wire, one 2" (5cm) piece of 16-gauge wire, one 3" (7.5cm) piece of 16-gauge wire, one 12" (30.5cm) piece of 26-gauge wire, one 18" (45.5cm) piece of 26-gauge wire, and one 26" (66cm) piece of 26-gauge wire.

Cut four 2-link pieces of chain and one 9-link piece of chain.

Select 12 carnelian, 7 labrodorite, and 5 garnet beads and organize from light to dark to create an ombré effect.

TO MAKE

1 Follow step 1 of the looped-ends horseshoe frame instructions. With round-nose pliers, make a simple loop on each end of the 1½" (3.8cm) piece of 16-gauge wire. Place the ½" (13mm) mandrel at the wire's center. (Both looped ends should be facing away from the center of the mandrel.) With your fingers, gently bend the wire around the mandrel. (This is the curved top piece of the frame.)

2 Repeat step 1 with the 2" (5cm) piece of 16-gauge wire and the ¾" (2cm) mandrel. (This is the middle piece of the frame.)

   Repeat step 1 with the 3" (7.5cm) piece of 16-gauge wire and the 1" (2.5cm) mandrel. (This is the bottom piece of the frame.)

3 Place all 3 frame pieces on the anvil and hammer each piece flat, being careful to hammer the loops only lightly.

4   Place the 26" (66cm) piece of 26-gauge wire at a loop on the bottom piece of frame and wrap the wire 5 times. Slide a bead onto the wire to nestle against the flattened part of the frame and wrap 3 times. Continue adding beads using the technique of wrapping single beads until you reach the end of the frame (about 12 beads), wrapping 3 times between beads. After the last bead, wrap the wire 5 times around the frame to secure. With wire cutters, trim the excess wire. With chain-nose pliers, pinch the wire tightly to the frame.

5   Repeat step 4 with the middle frame piece and the 18" (45.5cm) piece of 26-gauge wire, wrapping about 8 beads to the frame. Repeat step 4 with the top frame piece and the 12" (30.5cm) piece of 26-gauge wire, wrapping about 13 beads to the frame. With wire cutters, trim the excess wire on both pieces. With chain-nose pliers, pinch the wire tightly to the frame on both pieces.

6   With chain-nose pliers, gently open the loops on both sides of the bottom frame piece by twisting them to the side. Insert a 2-link piece of chain onto each loop. Close the loops.

7   With chain-nose pliers, gently open the loops on both sides of the middle frame piece by twisting them to the side. Insert a 2-link piece of chain and an end link of the chain attached to the bottom frame piece onto each loop. Close the loops.

8   With chain-nose pliers, gently open the loops on both sides of the top frame piece by twisting them to the side. Insert an end link of the 9-link piece of sturdy chain and an end of the chain attached to the middle frame piece onto each loop. Close the loops.

9   Attach an ear wire to the middle link (the 5th link) of the 9-link piece of sturdy chain.

10 Repeat steps 1–9 to make the second earring.

chain reaction

When using chain to create dangles for your earrings, remember to use an odd number of chain links. You will need one center link to attach the ear wire, allowing an even number of links to hang on both sides of the chain. As you work, take care that the chain does not twist around on itself, as this action can throw your entire design off center.

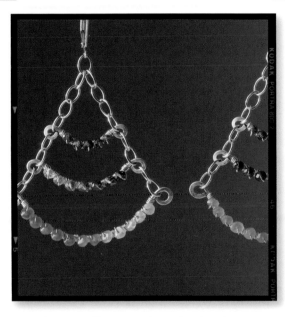

Note: If you would like your earrings to be mirror images, as shown, rather than matching, reverse the order in which you wrap beads in steps 4–5 for the second earring frame.

THE NEXT STEP: *Designing Earrings on Your Own*

After you've become familiar with the materials, tools, and techniques in this book, you'll be ready to create earrings of your own design. To get started, practice personalizing your favorite designs. The more comfortable you feel making changes to these designs, the easier it will be to start from scratch with raw materials.

Sometimes, a design will seem to pop into your brain fully formed. And sometimes it will take a bit more work. The creative process can be complicated! I wish I could wave a magic wand and say, "Okay, now you will be incredibly inventive and creative!" If I had had that wand, I would have saved myself years of frustration and anxiety as I tried to communicate my ideas through wire and stone, sometimes succeeding and sometimes failing. A few "rules" developed from those years of experience, and I like to remind myself of the following when I am working on new projects.

1 TRUST YOURSELF AND KEEP THE CHANNEL OPEN.

Everyone is creative. Everyone played with crayons when he or she were little, or finger-painted, or glued glitter onto paper, or made macaroni necklaces. We all created something that made us proud. When we get older, we learn to judge ourselves. I don't know when it happens. We judge ourselves on so many levels, often shutting down the creative forces that once flowed so freely. I hope you don't judge yourself while playing with this book. Instead, trust yourself and your creative instincts. Listen to your intuition and just go for it. The design might be a complete mess, but I guarantee you'll learn something in the process that will make your next pair of earrings better.

2 DON'T LEAVE YOUR WORK SPACE UNTIL YOU HAVE PUT IN SOME SERIOUS TIME.

In the beginning it is so easy to get frustrated and want to quit—or to distract yourself with some unnecessary task, such as cleaning out your refrigerator or reorganizing your sock drawer. You know what I mean?

My creative process is not the most glamorous, and with work and a family, I have to plan ahead and squeeze in time to create when I can. I begin by neatly arranging my materials in front of me. I pick up my tools, move some of the materials around and I wait, and I wait, and I wait. And I move some more materials around in a different way, get an idea, *hate* that idea, and take it all apart. (This is why I suggest designing in craft wire).

What I have learned is that if I wait it out, something magical will happen. Some insight will blossom, and the materials will come together in a way that is pleasing to me. I may not finish a design all in one sitting, but I will have a direction. Greatness, and great design, comes to those who wait and work it through.

3 DON'T EXPECT TODAY TO FEEL THE SAME AS YESTERDAY.

Moods change. Energy shifts. Yesterday, new ideas flowed. Today, you're stuck. Don't hold on to yesterday, and don't dread tomorrow. Approach and respect each day as it is.

4 DON'T BE AFRAID TO EXPERIMENT, AND DON'T BE AFRAID TO TAKE THINGS APART.

My design philosophy is to put items together, take them apart, and put them together in a new way until they make sense, which is why I always begin my designs in craft wire. That way, if my materials look horrible together, I feel no remorse about cutting up my design and starting over again.

5 PAY ATTENTION AND TAKE NOTES.

Okay, you sit and you think and you work, and after some time, you have an amazing earring design. But how did you get there?

Take it from me, there is nothing more deflating than realizing you have no idea what you did to make your final earring design. It makes sense to take notes as you go: How much wire did you cut? What gauge wire? Did you bend it before you added the bead? Did you work-harden the wire? What are the steps from A to Z that you need to remember so you can make it again? Keep a notebook on your worktable and write them down.

I work out of the same notebook I have been working with for ten years. It's my go-to resource when I am stuck and struggling. It contains information on past designs and inspirations and serves as a record of the evolution of my designs.

6 JUST START.

ENOUGH SAID.

CARING FOR YOUR EARRINGS

You'll want to take the best possible care of your new earring creations. Storing and cleaning your earrings properly will extend their life and keep them looking just as beautiful as they were the day you made them. Below I offer a few suggestions on how to care for and clean your fabulous new jewelry.

HOW TO STORE YOUR EARRINGS

Just as it is never good to throw a pair of earrings into your purse, where they can be tangled, maimed, scratched, and twisted, throwing your earrings into a drawer doesn't do much good for them, either. Haphazard or careless storage can spell disaster for your handmade accessories. Beads will scratch and chip; wire will snag, tangle, and bend out of shape. You could even lose one half of a favorite pair.

There are two ways to store your jewelry: visibly, using your jewelry as works of art to decorate your house, or invisibly, protecting your jewelry from light and dust. Either way works, and I do both, as I have *a lot* of jewelry—some I like to look at all the time and others I protect.

My toddler *loves* to play in my jewelry, so the good pieces have to stay out of sight and reach. I found an inexpensive solution at my local organization store using wire cabinet shelving. I simply clip my earrings to each other (most of my earrings are leverback, which makes this possible) and lay them on a bar, each earring straddling a side. I can store a ton of earrings on one rack easily with a high degree of visibility. If you don't want to sacrifice cabinet space, it's fine to store your jewelry in a drawer, but purchase or make drawer dividers that will keep each pair separate. Or you could even place each pair of earrings in a plastic bag and designate one part of your drawer for Everyday Chic, another for Bohemian Beauty, and so on. By keeping each pair of earrings together, you'll be able to quickly find just the right pair to complement whatever the look of the day happens to be.

Of course, I like to look at pretty things, and keeping some of my jewelry visible makes me happy. My favorite way to store earrings is to clip them together in pairs and then scatter them in vintage bowls, dishes, and plates. The whole collection just glitters and sparkles and is really fun to have around.

HOW TO CLEAN YOUR EARRINGS

I wear my earrings everywhere. I wear earrings to work, out to dinner with friends, on playdates with my son—I even wear my earrings while taking yoga classes. Hey, a girl must accessorize! Needless to say, my earrings can get kind of gritty—and there is a proper way to clean them.

The cheap and easy way to clean gemstone-based earrings: In a small bowl, mix mild dish soap and warm water. Dip your jewelry into this solution and swish it around. (You can also use a nonabrasive jewelry cleaner if you choose.) Remove it and rinse in warm running water. Gently buff dry with a soft, lint-free cloth, and *voilà!* Shiny, clean jewels! This works well with gold and gold-filled earrings, and with all types of gemstone beads.

The cheap and easy way to clean sterling silver earrings: Purchase a nonabrasive silver polishing cloth. There are many different kinds on the market, and they should not cost you more than $5 each. Buff the silver with the polishing cloth and you're done!

RESOURCES

All of the projects in this book call for materials that are readily available at jewelry supply or craft stores near you. If you have trouble finding a product or material, consult the websites listed below.

MATERIALS AND TOOLS

www.ABeadStore.com
beads, wire, chain, findings, and tools

www.ArtBeads.com
beads, wire, findings, and tools

www.ArtCraftWire.com
craft wire

www.Beadaholique.com
beads, wire, chain, findings, and tools

www.BeadIt.com
beads

www.BHBeads.com
beads, wire, chain, findings, and tools

www.FireMountainGems.com
beads, wire, chain, findings, and tools

www.firemountaingems.com/encyclobeadia/beading_resources.p?docid=BEADHOLESIZES
(for bead hole size chart)

www.GemMall.com
beads, wire, findings, and tools

www.GoodyBeads.com
beads, wire, chain, findings, and tools

www.HouseofGems.com
beads, wire, chain, findings, and tools

www.JewelrySupply.com
beads, wire, findings, chain, and tools

www.Joann.com
embroidery thread, beads, wire, chain, findings, and tools

www.KamalTrading.com
wire, chain, findings, and Swarovski crystal

www.Kreinik.com
embroidery thread

www.LimaBeads.com

www.Michaels.com
beads, wire, chain, findings, and tools

www.RioGrande.com
beads, wire, chain, findings, and tools

www.ShipwreckBeads.com
beads, wire, chain, findings, and tools

www.SIIFindings.com

www.TheBeadinPath.com
beads, wire, findings, chain, and tools

ABOUT THE AUTHOR

Stephanie A. Wells is the founder and creator of Double Happiness Jewelry, a California-based jewelry company that has proven to be a favorite of celebrities, their stylists, and fashion magazine editors. Her story began with a fierce obsession with gemstones, a love for making jewelry, and countless nights spent in her garage creating unique earrings to express her sense of style. Beseeched by strangers, friends, and storeowners to sell her designs, Wells produced her first collection. Her sister, Alisa Rottenberg, sold the pieces on the streets of New York, finding a place for Double Happiness Jewelry to debut on a New York City runway.

Today, Double Happiness Jewelry is sold in more than 400 stores worldwide, and pieces from the company's collections are featured monthly in major international fashion magazines, including *Elle*, *InStyle*, *Cosmopolitan*, *Vogue*, *Harper's BAZAAR*, and *Lucky*. Celebrity clients include Oprah Winfrey, Jessica Simpson, Alicia Keys, Tyra Banks, Britney Spears, Rachael Ray, and Beyoncé. Wells's latest endeavor, Elli by Double Happiness Jewelry, is a direct sales complement to the business and allows men and women to sell their favorite Double Happiness Jewelry collections through home parties.

Wells lives in San Diego with her husband and young son. Visit her online at doublehappinessjewelry.com and elli.com.

INDEX